Writing Television & Motion Picture Scripts That Sell

Evelyn Goodman

Contemporary Books, Inc.
Chicago

Library of Congress Cataloging in Publication Data

Goodman, Evelyn.
 Writing television and motion picture scripts that sell.

 Includes index.
 1. Television authorship.   2. Moving-picture authorship.   I. Title.
PN1992.7.G63   808'.02   81-69626
ISBN 0-8092-5787-4 (pbk.)   AACR2

207405

Published by Contemporary Books, Inc.
180 North Michigan Avenue, Chicago, Illinois 60601
Manufactured in the United States of America
Library of Congress Catalog Card Number: 81-69626
International Standard Book Number: 0-8092-5787-4 (paper)

Published simultaneously in Canada by
Beaverbooks, Ltd.
150 Lesmill Road
Don Mills, Ontario M3B 2T5
Canada

Contents

1

The Overview

Writing the teleplay or screenplay is a specialized form of writing. The reader of the novel can read a page or a chapter at will, either a few pages or a chapter at a time, put the book down, and resume reading the next day or next week. In contrast, the script for the television or motion picture theater screen must capture the viewer's interest at once and sustain that interest to the fadeout—the final one. But the first test of whether the work is succeeding is whether it will sell.

What makes the teleplay or screenplay work? What makes the script salable? The essential ingredients for one are the same for the other. The motion picture script and the teleplay must catch and hold interest in one way only—through sight and sound. You, the writer, must tell your story so that it plays on screen. That is the discipline of writing for the motion picture or home screen. It is a craft, and for the writer who sets out to learn the craft and learn it well, it can be very lucrative.

This book will take you step by step through the process of creating the teleplay and screenplay. Basically, the structuring is similar for both of them. A major difference is in the type of material each requires for its audience. Whether to write for one or the other depends on you. Many writers work in both areas. The opportunities are there, currently greater than ever before—with excellent payment.

First, let's look at the screenplay.

THE EVOLUTION OF THE SCREENPLAY

An original screenplay can sell for as much as $300,000 or $400,000, and new writers with no previous screenplay credits at all or even any past professional writing credits have made that first big sale. The six-figure sale does not happen often. Indeed, the percentage is small, considering the number of original screenplays written. In 1981 alone more than eight thousand screenplays were registered with the Writers Guild of America West (WGA West) Registration Service. But that productivity points out the awareness of writers to the opportunities in motion pictures to sell the original screenplay—opportunities that up until the last dozen years did not exist.

Paul Schrader sold his original screenplay *Yakuza,* a first for him, for $300,000. *The Sting,* an original screenplay, sold for $400,000. At that time David Ward, too, was unknown, making his first screenplay sale. William Goldman earned $400,000 for his original *Butch Cassidy and the Sundance Kid.*

Yet there was a time when original screenplays were not considered at all. Screenwriters were hired by the major studios to adapt presold successful material such as the best-selling novel or the hit Broadway play. Then how did it happen that the industry—which had always been slavish to presold, proven material to be adapted to the screen—should turn about and welcome original screenplays?

The economics of the industry changed. Picture production in the major studios drastically declined, and the majors did not have exclusivity in filmmaking any longer. By the mid-sixties, a new breed of filmmaker, the independent, was becoming entrenched in the business of moviemaking.

It was the independent who recognized the genuine cost advantage in the purchase of the original screenplay instead of paying first for the big book or hit play and then having to hire a screenwriter. Francis Ford Coppola, of *The Godfather* and *Apocalypse Now* fame, was one of the young independent producers with *You're a Big Boy Now*. He also wrote the screenplay.

Of the screenplays fashioned out of novels, *The Graduate* and *Midnight Cowboy* were among the more successful, with *Midnight Cowboy* also winning an Oscar for Waldo Salt for writing the best screenplay adapted from another medium. The James Bond movies, adapted from the Ian Fleming novels, struck a popular audience response with *Dr. No,* the first to be made into a film. The fare was varied—suspense, adventure, drama, comedy—all types.

THE NEW TREND—LOW BUDGET

Then something happened that surprised the motion picture industry. In fact, it was a stunning surprise. *Easy Rider* rode across the screen depicting a cross section of America of the time—the sixties—and created a sensation. It was a phenomenon.

Budgeted on a shoestring, it became a box office success. Peter Fonda and Dennis Hopper, the writers, co-stars, and producers, both of whom were virtually unknown at the time, wrote much of *Easy Rider* as they were filming it during their motorcycle cross-country travel, around which the story revolves.

This picture also introduced Jack Nicholson as another "easy rider." Although his character dies early in the film, Nicholson's outstanding performance as a cynical lawyer-turned-counterculture motorbiker launched him on the road to stardom.

This low-budget blockbuster set up a clamor in the studios among all the producers for another *Easy Rider*. Everyone wanted to make a low-budget original just like this big runaway success. What kind of picture is it?

The form of *Easy Rider* is episodic, a slender story line threaded all through it giving it the cohesiveness that binds the series of episodes into the meaningful whole. Audiences could identify strongly with it because it captures the spirit and dispirit of the sixties—the violence, the assassinations, the protests, the Vietnam War, the Civil Rights movement, the struggle to gain a foothold—all the dissatisfactions out of which the love-peace movements sprang as the counteraction. The type of audience had also changed to a younger one, ranging in age from eighteen to twenty-five. The older person was, supposedly, at home watching television.

The Waning Cycle

In jumping on the low-budget bandwagon, new independent filmmakers sprang up from everywhere to make pictures in any inexpensive space available. But the approach to making films emphasized a slipshod concept of stringing episodes together on a contemporary theme. What was overlooked was the fine quality of *Easy Rider* and its cohesiveness.

Most of these low-budget pictures attempting to imitate *Easy Rider* failed. One of the better ones was *Alice's Restaurant,* starring Arlo Guthrie, who also wrote and produced it. But *Five Easy Pieces,* screenplay by Carol Eastman and starring Jack Nicholson, was the strongest of all the modest-priced productions. By then, audiences were bored with the formless films. Although *Five Easy Pieces* was the oasis in the desert and heralded by the critics, it appeared too late to revitalize the dying low-budget, episodic cycle.

UNSUCCESSFUL TRENDS

Meanwhile, Eric Segal had written an original screenplay, *Love Story,* and for two years tried in vain to sell it. No one believed that the hip audiences of the day would accept a romantic rich boy/poor girl movie, as disconnected from the realities of the times as a fairy tale. Segal had greater faith in *Love Story* and in himself, and from his screenplay, he fashioned a novel. *Love Story,* as a book, became a best-seller. A motion picture sale at a handsome price was easily effected.

The movie, with Ryan O'Neal and Ali McGraw as the lovers, broke box office records. A new trend emerged. This time every studio and every producer wanted another love story. But a new cycle failed to develop for lack of love story motion picture material of the quality and appeal of the original *Love Story*.

During this time there were waves of popular pictures, such as those starring Clint Eastwood. This star has a big following for all his pictures, which are also generally well made. Paul Newman and Robert Redford played Butch Cassidy and the Sundance Kid in the smash hit of that name. Although considered two of the handful of top-rated Golden Boys of the Screen, they did not combine their talents again until *The Sting*.

The Sam Peckinpah cultists are cash customers for his violent films. The Bruce Lee action-packed karate films also proved popular, and *Yakuza,* dealing with Japanese martial arts, rode the crest of that trend. Paul Schrader had written his original screenplay *Taxi Driver* before *Yakuza,* but could not sell it until he made the *Yakuza* sale, a handsome $350,000 one. Within a year of his first big screen credit, his original screenplay sales made him a millionaire, and, as has happened to other writers after at least one big credit, he became director and producer of his own pictures.

David Ward's original script for *The Sting* garnered him $400,000. William Goldman got an equal amount for writing *Butch Cassidy and the Sundance Kid.*

Hello, Dolly!, the Broadway musical smash hit starring Carol Channing, was made into a musical costing $8,000,000. The motion picture industry was reaching for the blockbuster, the runaway success, and keen industry attention was focused on the film fate of *Hello, Dolly!*

The major studios were stepping back into filmmaking. But there was no answer yet as to whether it was wise to spend millions on a film unless it proved highly profitable. If *Hello, Dolly!* packed the movie theaters, then, after a long hiatus, musical pictures would be in the forefront of motion picture making. But the moviegoers' response did not warrant the money spent on it. A musical cycle was not established, a "That's Entertainment" era not reborn.

A NEW CYCLE—DISASTER

The great runaway success did happen. It taxied off the runway as a jumbo jet and climbed into the clouds with a full load of passengers and something extra—a bomb. A thrill-packed, spine-tingling story was unfolding on screen. *Airport* made motion picture history for its all-time record-breaking box office receipts, only to be exceeded by a new series of big pictures and their record-shattering revenues.

In the industry, *Airport* was categorized as a "disaster" film—the first of the disaster cycle. Then the call went out for disaster films, the bigger the better, never mind the costs. As the disaster films continued with one success topping another, the industry rule of thumb that the bigger the picture the more money it made was proving correct.

The Poseidon Adventure was another profitable disaster film that turned a cruise ship upside down in a tidal wave. *Earthquake* thundered across big screens in Sensurround, destroying Los Angeles in measured intervals of increasing violence. During the lulls in nature's devastation, the time was used for the personal storylines to develop in terms of rising conflict and the other essentials of an unfolding screenplay.

All these pictures were based on well-written screenplays. Even though the buildings collapsed, as in *Earthquake,* the production was not created on a quicksand script. The writer who invented a good original disaster screenplay could find eager buyers.

But in this market of rapidly devouring disasters, whatever looked like exceptional material was bought. *Airport,* which began it all, stemmed from a best-selling novel. Flames engulfing a skyscraper endangered the lives of guests gathered for a party in *The Towering Inferno,* a motion picture adapted from two novels: *The Tower,* by Richard Martin Stern, and *The Glass Inferno,* by Frank M. Robinson.

As disaster piled on disaster, it became evident to studios that there were only so many disasters in the world, and they could run thin. But out of the ocean depths swam a killer shark. Audiences jammed the movie houses to see *Jaws.* Universal Studios spent $6,000,000 on the construction of the shark. *Jaws* justified all the huge expense in the making of the movie. It became the all-time grosser, its success surpassing all its predecessors.

SUPERNATURAL SUCCESS

Even with all the crashing, burning, and shark mangling, the supernatural also caught the public's fancy. *The Exorcist* drew long lines of customers into the theaters. The supernatural-horror trend was initiated. But although producers sought more pictures in that genre, the good material was not forthcoming. It was hard to find original screenplays or books for adaptation that looked like motion picture winners.

A number of attempts at another *Exorcist* failed. So did *Exorcist II,* the sequel to the successful first film. Only two movies of the supernatural-horror type did succeed. The modestly budgeted *Carrie* became the sleeper of the year. *The Omen,* an original screenplay by David Seltzer starring Gregory Peck, was such a hit it set studios seeking another. At the time, however, another *Omen* did not materialize. For that reason, a supernatural-horror cycle was not set in motion as had happened with the disaster films. There were not enough films of this nature that worked.

A NEW HIT

Audience interest in the disaster film waned, and already filmgoers were welcoming another type of picture—*Rocky*. This human, heartwarming picture about a loser whose life was changed by a challenge that gave him hope and the incentive to win, earned an Oscar for Sylvester Stallone, who wrote the original screenplay and starred in the movie.

SCIENCE FICTION

Action-adventure in outer space whirled the filmgoer once again into the super-thrills and spine tingles of sheer entertainment. *Star Wars,* from the richly imaginative original screenplay by George Lucas (who also produced it), soared into spectacular success. Costing $40,000,000 to make, its huge revenues quickly put it high on the profit side of the ledger. The call was out for more science fiction. *Close Encounters of the Third Kind,* written and directed by Steven Spielberg, was ready for release and enjoyed substantial popularity, due in large measure to its special effects. The landing of the spacecraft at the end of the film is a memorable achievement in itself.

Other spacecraft rocketed toward other planets. Some did not make it, losing altitude and dropping to dismal earthly box office receipts. *Star Trek* as a motion picture was not a winner, while *Buck Rogers in the 25th Century* was popular with movie audiences. However, when it became a television series, it did not sustain itself.

Then it became time for *Superman.* Audiences delighted in seeing the mighty Man of Steel zooming over Metropolis in his search for archvillain Lex Luthor and then spinning around the world in his race with time to stop the madman's scheme. The popularity of *Superman*—even the mention of the name has a magical quality—overcame the flawed screenplay, an original which collaborator Mario Puzo (famed author of the novel *The Godfather*) shared with three other writers.

The Black Hole, a Walt Disney Production, and George Lucas's *The Empire Strikes Back* proved highly profitable. *Alien,* a mixed bag of horror in outer space, based on an original screenplay, is another winner in the box office sweepstakes, demonstrating again the public taste in filmgoing for new thrills and new excitement of a purely escapist nature.

MANY VARIETIES

This does not exclude other values. At the present time, with no new runaway cycle flooding the screens, quite a diversified moviegoing menu is being offered. However, there are groupings of subjects that carry interest, particularly the Vietnam War. During the unpopular war, the industry shied away from making pictures about it. A rare exception, and in a heroic vein, was *The Green Berets,* culled from the book of that title. Since the war's end, aspects of the grim conflict have been exposed in some excellent films, namely, *Coming Home,* which won best performance Oscars for Jane Fonda and Jon Voight; *The Deer Hunter;* and *Apocalypse Now,* the Francis Ford Coppola epic for which Joseph Conrad's *Heart of Darkness* served as the basis of John Milius's screenplay. *Coming Home* is from an original screenplay by Nancy Dowd. *The Deerhunter* screenplay is adapted from the book of that name. *Heroes,* starring Henry Winkler, preceded these films as the first in movie houses focusing on the war; Winkler enacted the role of a Vietnam veteran returning home.

Dracula films also became quite prevalent in the movie theaters, with *Love at First Bite* (original screenplay by Robert Kaufman) and *Dracula* (based loosely on the Bram Stoker book), two of the well-received Dracula pictures.

A mild Sherlock Holmes resurgence resulted from the popularity of Nicholas Meyer's *The Seven-Per-Cent Solution.*

Suspense, murder mysteries, comedies, and solid, hard-hitting dramas such as *North Dallas Forty* gave filmgoers a wide variety from which to choose.

Since the successes of *Julia* and *The Turning Point,* women stars have been more visible on the screen. Those who rank in the Golden class include Liza Minnelli, Jane Fonda, Barbra Streisand, and Faye Dunaway. This category parallels that of the Golden Boys, and the screenplay offering such star roles stands a chance of capturing prize money.

Westerns, which had once been a mainstay of television and motion pictures, decreased in popularity to almost nonexistence on the screen. Michael Cimino's motion picture *Heaven's Gate,* costing $46,000,000, was not well received either in the first version that opened in New York (where it quickly closed), or in the cut, revised version that opened at the Filmex (International) Film Exposition in Hollywood. Nor has a Western trend developed. The motion picture *Outland* has won favor, but its Western-type story, marshal and all, is set on another planet. Generally, filmgoers today are far more receptive to science fiction than horse hooves pounding on dusty trails, and prefer other high adventure in the tempo of the times.

Two of the hits at this writing are *Superman II,* a film superior to *Superman,* and *Raiders of the Lost Ark,* with screenplay by Lawrence Kasden, produced by George Lucas, and directed by Steven Spielberg. Horror films are still very marketable. However, at any given time, a new trend might develop by virtue of something new and different capturing public fancy. Such is the nature of cycles.

The new technologies will greatly increase the demand for original screenplays. But remember, if you want to ride in on the crest of a trend, do not wait to offer your original screenplay at the beginning of the end of the cycle. Know what motion picture material is selling. Be alert for any new development in moviemaking. It may be that your original screenplay starts a trend. But if your theme is not in the mainstream of what is being bought, the odds are that it will not attract as quick a sale as the screenplay that hits the market on target. Of course, you must do your very best to present a well-written screenplay.

The opportunity is there; it is exciting and challenging for the writer of the original screenplay. And for the screenwriter who rides into a big trend and offers the extra-plus feature of a role for one of the Golden stars, the sale price can be well into the six-figure range. But do not designate one particular star in writing your screenplay. That star may not be available.

Those are prospects for the big screen. Now let's look at the home screen.

TELEVISION—HOW SHOWS ARE DETERMINED

Unlike the motion picture industry, where box office receipts can be used as the gauge of successes and failures, commercial television bases its financing on advertising revenues—that is, commercials. To determine how many prospective customers are viewing each show, advertisers rely on the rating system. This also is a decisive factor for the networks in determining what shows are bought, renewed, or canceled.

Best known of the demographics specialists of this type is the A. C. Nielsen Co., which conducts a rating system that is the bible of the industry. A selected number of families throughout the nation are picked, with their permission, as barometers. What they are viewing on television during a given time is judged to be the national taste. Sponsors or prospective sponsors are convinced that they can determine the number of consumers who are buying or will buy their various products by the number of people selected for the Nielsen viewing test who are watching the shows on which their products are advertised. If the ratings slip badly or never build up, shows are canceled.

Once in a while, a new show is a slow starter, but the network executives have enough faith in it to give it a chance. "The Waltons" was one such show. For nearly a year, its sluggish ratings hung the Sword of Damocles over its head. But CBS television executives did give the show enough time to build, and as it climbed in popularity to a top ten rating, the Walton family was adopted into a large proportion of families in America.

THE SHOWS SET IN TIME PATTERNS

These shows offer the writer a different type of market than that of motion pictures. Television is a precise medium, working on a time schedule. The types of shows you write for are set for you by time patterns, and it is up to you to decide which show you prefer and which is the best for expressing your talent. For instance, if your forte is comedy, would it not be wiser for you to put your best foot forward writing a sit-com (situation comedy) than trying a detective-mystery show?

The sit-coms are mainly half hour shows because it was found that they work better in the shorter time period. They are series shows with established characters who, if the show is a popular one, are regular visitors into the home week after week.

"The Dick Van Dyke Show" and "The Bob Newhart Show" had long staying power. "The Mary Tyler Moore Show" is seen regularly in syndication reruns, as are other shows that achieved considerable popularity.

However, of the 22 new shows of the 1979–80 season, 11 were situation comedies. Not many survived the season. "Taxi" was one of the few successful new sit-coms. "The Jeffersons," a popular veteran sit-com, enjoyed new success by moving up to top position in the ratings. But since sit-coms are a staple on series television, the 1980–81 season premiered a new rash of them. As in the 1979–80 season, survivors could be counted on fingers. "The Jeffersons" continued in first place in ratings week after week, while "M*A*S*H" played tag with that top position in sustaining its long-run popularity. "House Calls" was one of the well-received new sit-coms. "Diff'rent Strokes," premiering the season before, continued to hold viewers.

"Three's Company," "Barney Miller," "Taxi," and "Laverne and Shirley" were other sit-coms that sustained their long-run popularity into the 1980–81 season, although "Three's Company" had slipped from the top ten ratings that it had previously enjoyed. "Mork and Mindy," which had leaped into immediate top-rated popularity when it first premiered, also dropped considerably in the ratings. As one of the survivors beginning the 1981–82 season at this writing, the show is undergoing a number of changes. "Mork and Mindy" will marry and have a baby. But the childbearing roles will be reversed, with Mork giving birth to an offspring who is predetermined to be not a bouncing baby boy, but a grown man—a role that Jonathan Winters will play. For on the planet Ork, as Mork explains, children are born old and grow young. If the show survives that long, Mork and Mindy may yet become parents of an infant son.

"Archie Bunker's Place" sustained popularity well into the 1980–81 season after Jean Stapleton left "All in the Family" and the show was revised into "Archie Bunker's Place." It is renewed for 1981–82.

However, the entire picture of sit-coms has changed considerably. In a reversal of the past two seasons, 1981–82 is no longer emphasizing these half-hour television comedies. They are still a staple on the networks. But more hour shows are on the schedules.

The hour show is the longer series type, with such variations as action-melodrama, drama, and comedy-drama. This includes such shows as "Quincy," "Lou Grant," "Hart to Hart," and "Trapper John, M.D." Medical shows as well as lawyer shows have dwindled in numbers on television. That doctor-lawyer cycle, once so popular on television, shows no signs of a resurgence in the 1981–82 schedules. "Trapper John, M.D." is sustaining popularity, and "Nurse," which joined the diminishing hospital genre this past season, is also renewed for the new season.

Indeed, the type of hour series changes from season to season, depending on ratings and what is judged as popular with viewers. When Westerns vanished from the television screen with "Gunsmoke," the last and longest-run Western series canceled in the early 1970s, a new cycle, the "cop" shows, ruled the screen, such as "The Streets of San Francisco," "Hawaii Five-O," and "Kojak." But protests by civic groups over what they regarded as violence on television, combined with waning viewer interest, reduced the number of police and private investigator (private-eye) shows. However, detective and suspense shows have a built-in viewing interest and can return in larger proportions at any given time.

At this writing, the 1981–82 season is offering a resurgence of the detective and "cop" shows and also of favorite stars of past series. James Arness, the famed Matt Dillon of "Gunsmoke," returns as a detective in "McClain's Law," and Rock Hudson will star as a detective in "Devlin Connection." Angie Dickinson will be seen as the star of a new private eye show known as "Cassie & Co.," and Robert Stack of "The Untouchables," will head the new "Strike Force." Other stars on TV shows will be Mike Connors in "Today's FBI" and James Garner in a new "Maverick" series. Although not a "Six Million Dollar Man," Lee Majors is destined for high action as a stunt man in "The Fall Guy," in pursuit of bail jumpers. Lorne Greene has already premiered in "Code Red," centered on fire department activity. And there are still others of this action-suspense genre scheduled, giving the new 1981–82 season a lively cops-and-robbers type look. How this new deluge of detective-police shows will fare is at this writing unpredictable. But it is likely that the stars will attract the viewers. Of course, good scripts are a top attraction, too!

The two-hour television script, the feature for television (i.e., television movie), is another form that has gained a strong foothold on the home screen. The two-hour movie made for television is anthological in nature, and tells a complete story as a motion picture does, but does not carry series characters.

When the features made for television were first introduced, ninety minutes was the desirable length, but the longer form gained in popularity. An even longer form became the miniseries, which had its premiere with *Rich Man, Poor Man,* adapted from Irwin Shaw's novel and shown in sections continuously over several nights.

The miniseries, adaptations from best-selling novels—and sometimes books that did not make a best-seller list—caught the public fancy. *Roots* broke all ratings records every night a new segment of it was shown. *Holocaust* proved another big winner.

Currently, however, interest in miniseries productions is diminishing: Once the novelty wore off, the viewing public became too impatient to stay with any miniseries (short of a blockbuster), night after night. Nor can the viewers be counted on to pick up a new segment of the miniseries a week later, or even two days later, if that time lapse is allowed. This again points up the constant search for new patterns in entertainment and the establishment of a new cycle once a certain type of show has proved successful.

Nothing, however, can remain constant, because the economics of the industry won't allow it. The advertisers and their commercials pay the bills. They don't buy into or continue to support a show that does badly in the ratings. Anyway, the miniseries offers little market for the new writer. Adaptations are assigned to established writers, just as pilots for new shows are generally assigned to the writers with the credits or, as it is called in the industry, the track records.

Whatever weekly series show you decide to write for, know the show. Watch the show at least three times before you begin your writing. Know the general format, the characters, the flavor of the dialogue. And, a word of caution: Do not attempt to change the image of an established series character, for these characters, particularly the stars, have been molded to fit that particular type of series.

Of course, the feature for television gives you a free hand in creating your own characters. But you should watch the features to see the types of stories that are making the sales. Watch features for the writing techniques. As you study the following chapters, you will understand better what makes a good script; you will also know when a script does not hold your interest, and you will understand why.

ECONOMIC REWARDS

Prices for the scripts make it well worth the effort. The new Writers Guild of America minimums, set as a result of the settlement of a three-month strike by WGA members, are at the highest ever for writers in the television and motion picture industry. All the more gratifying for writers is that the new WGA 1981 Theatrical and Television Basic Agreement, a four-year pact, also has the unprecedented provision for writers of profit sharing on scripts for pay-TV (cable), videocassettes, and videodiscs. These new technologies are fast gaining popularity and are offering tremendous new market potentials for writers.

The new WGA script fee minimums follow: for the sale of the thirty-minute television script, $7,548; for the sale of the one-hour original teleplay, $10,566; for the ninety-minute teleplay, $15,094; and for the two-hour teleplay sale, $18,868. These minimums are for the outright sale of television scripts of these various lengths. Prices became effective retroactively from March 2, 1981.

The new fee structure also provides for a 12 percent script fee increase effective July 1, 1982, an 11 percent increase effective July 1, 1983, and a 9 percent increase effective July 1, 1984. An additional 4 percent is effective on the 1984 date for teleplays over sixty minutes, which is designated as *long form*.

The sale of the high-budget screenplay now carries the WGA minimum price tag of $29,485, with yearly increases advancing the price to $40,000 effective July 1, 1984. As discussed earlier, original screenplays for motion pictures have sold for as much as six-figure prices, depending on the script and if a major star is engaged. Although minimum fees are set in regard to selling the screenplay, there is no ceiling on the maximum in either motion pictures or in television. Generally, a first script in television obtains for the new writer the basic minimum.

Initial script fees for productions for pay-TV, videocassettes, and videodiscs are 100 percent of the minimums of free-TV plus the profit-sharing terms for writers. The WGA basic agreement also incorporated in the contract sets these payments: 2 percent of gross after recoupment in tape based on $1,000,000 per hour and 2 percent of gross in film based on recoupment of $1,250,000 per hour. A scale of increases in also set, with an increase of the profit sharing percentage of 12 percent, 11 percent, and 9 percent on July 1, 1982, through July 1, 1984.

It is expected that new, original films will be sought for pay-TV, with a continuing expansion of independent producers as well as the major studios engaging in this production. Writers of television and motion picture scripts can look forward to vastly expanding markets for their work. There is no more opportune time than now for the writer of television and motion picture scripts that sell. Indeed, these are exciting, golden times in filmwriting fields, offering to the writer greater opportunities than ever before, with greater financial benefits.

Now you want to know how to write your script and to make it as good and as salable as possible.

2

Format—The Page Form

To get a firm understanding of the visual medium that will be the foundation of your writing for television and motion pictures, it is well that you first understand the page form of the script. Keep in mind that this is an entirely different form than for the printed page. Where the printed page is read and its meaning conveyed through the eye to the mind, the typewritten script page must translate into sight and sound. Note that you should always submit a *typewritten* script.

WHAT TO INCLUDE

Because you are conveying on the page only that which can be seen and heard (because your script is written to be played on the screen), the script you present, that you hope will be bought for production, must be written in scenes. The scenes must concentrate solely on dialogue and movement—the *sight* and *sound*. Scene writing is the only manner in which a script will be read as a vehicle for the screen.

Let's look then, at the essentials of the script page. Every script opens with FADE IN and ends with FADE OUT. At the start, the teleplay or motion picture is fading up from black and at the closing wipes again to black, thus the FADE IN and FADE OUT. But the teleplay, unlike the movie, is written with act breaks for commercials, and so each act closes on FADE OUT, with the following act opening on FADE IN. FADE IN and FADE OUT are typed in capital letters—CAPS.

Your next order of business is to describe the location of the scene. Because you are working in the visual, defining the location of each scene is essential. First, you must indicate in your script whether the scene is played inside (i.e., interior, such as in a living room or kitchen, bedroom, or office) or outside (i.e., exterior, such as the outdoor setting of garden, road, or beach). If the scene is INTERIOR, describe it as INT., and similarly, use EXT. as an abbreviation for *exterior* in the outdoor scene.

After you designate whether your scene is EXT. or INT., it is necessary to set the specific location and follow that with the time, DAY or NIGHT, all in caps. For example, if the scene is played at breakfast, in the kitchen of the home of Mr. and Mrs. Dallings, you will give the description of it in this manner: INT. KITCHEN OF DALLINGS' HOME—DAY.

Now you have established both the setting and time of the scene. But your script is not opening on an empty stage. You have to describe what is essential in that kitchen and the type of kitchen that fits your script and the Dallings' type of home.

THE TYPEWRITTEN PAGE

Whether for television or motion picture, this description is typed out, single-spaced, from margin to margin (i.e., across the page). Allow for a good inch-and-one-half margin when you type these directives on the left side of the page. You will also have typed your INT. or EXT. location placements on the left side, with the same allowance for margin.

But you go further in the set than the picture of the kitchen, for your scene also opens with the Dallings present. Therefore, it is necessary to describe them. The description will include their physical appearance and attire. It is not necessary to, nor should you, detail every inch of their appearance from head to toe, but only the pertinent points about them that you need in order to tell your story.

You describe the Dallings. But what are they doing? Your script now takes them into movement—action—and dialogue. Before Betty or Joe Dallings utters a word, each is doing something. For example, Joe Dallings is reading the morning paper at the breakfast table and drinking orange juice, while his wife is at the kitchen stove scrambling eggs. This becomes a single-spaced description, typed margin to margin, left to right, allowing for the same good left-hand margin and enough margin on the right-hand side, usually an inch and one-quarter.

Inevitably, a character speaks. This is where your script page takes on a strongly distinctive look that far removes it from anything resembling a printed page, because you now work in the center of the page. The character name is centered on the page in capital letters. Then, one space below the character name, you type in the dialogue. The dialogue is also typed out center page, but single-spaced.

As an example, Betty and Joe are engaged in a quarrel. Still busy at the kitchen stove, Betty accuses Joe of having flirted with another woman when they were out last night. Joe defends himself.

```
                    JOE
          I hardly looked at Lorraine
          at the party.

(Betty turns off the fire on the stove, wraps a pot
  cover over the handle of the frying pan, and walking
  to Joe with the frying pan, she thrusts it at his face.)


                   BETTY
          Then what were you doing
          sneaking out to the patio
          with her?
```

Note that Betty's action begins two spaces down from Joe's dialogue, and single-spaced. Always drop your writing down two spaces from the dialogue to the action description.

You may be writing this scene to lead up to a marital breakup between them, or, perhaps, a new understanding. Whatever the purpose for the scene, the completion of it requires a CUT TO for the transition to the next scene. CUT TO is typed in caps at the right side of the page up to the margin.

Moving on to the next scene again requires the description of location and time. However, if the EXT. scene plays in the same place, you may type in SAME but designate the time if there has been a shift (such as from DAY to NIGHT).

The entire filmed script plays forty-five seconds to a minute per page. Therefore, an hour script can take up from approximately fifty-six or fifty-seven pages to sixty-four. You will find a complete hour script in Chapter 7.

Although motion pictures do not have act breaks, the movie of average length, two hours, takes 120 pages of typewritten script. In all other respects except act breaks, as we have discussed, motion pictures follow the same page format as television films.

However, television situation comedy has a different format for the typewritten page. Because the sit-com plays a half hour with, generally, three sets (two the fixed sets for the weekly show), this type of show can be taped (found to be far more economical than filming) and calls for a different typing format. The action of the script for the taped show is typed not across the page from margin to margin, but covering three-quarters across, and it is typed in caps. The characters' names are centered within the three-quarters page span and in caps, as in the filmed script, but the dialogue, unlike in the filmed page, is double-spaced. Generally, the action is enclosed in parentheses.

For example:

                    JOE

        I hardly looked at Lorraine

        at the party.

    (BETTY TURNS OFF THE FIRE ON THE STOVE. WRAPS

    A POT COVER OVER THE HANDLE OF THE FRYING PAN,

    AND WALKING TO JOE WITH THE FRYING PAN, SHE

    THRUSTS IT AT HIS FACE.)

```
                BETTY

        (IN DEEP ANGER) Then what were

        you doing sneaking out to the patio

        with her?
```

It is interesting to note that this format is close to that of the teleplays that belonged to "Live from New York" in the 1950s. The "Live" script divided the page into two columns, one headed *Video* and the other *Audio*. Every line on either side was typed double-spaced, and the combination of both columns extended over three-quarters of the typewritten page. Although the format of audio and video columns is no longer used, the taped script, leaning closer to the live show than to film, borrows some of the format.

Note, too, that there is a difference in the number of script pages for the half-hour taped show and the filmed script. Although the half-hour show plays out its thirty minutes, including commercials, the number of typewritten pages does not conform to the typed filmed script because of the double-spacing. Therefore, the half-hour taped show runs anywhere from forty-two to forty-six typewritten pages.

These are the essentials for setting up your script pages. Remember: You are writing for sight and sound, and that compels the page form to be written scene by scene. You need not become involved in camera shots, for the director sets up each shot. Therefore, the writer has only a minimal interest in camera shots, primarily using master shots. In Chapter 9 we take up the subject of camera shots in greater detail.

Since there is no need to become particularly involved in camera shots, it is best now to concentrate on writing as good and salable a script as possible.

3

The Protagonist

To interest an audience, a teleplay or screenplay must contain a basic ingredient—*suspense*. No matter whether the television show or motion picture being viewed is comedy, drama, or melodrama, it must create in the viewer strong interest, scene by scene, in what will happen next. The viewer must care about the chief character and be so involved and concerned over whether he will attain his goal that interest remains active and solid. (The masculine pronoun is used only as a matter of convenience. As pointed out in Chapter 1, female leads are popular in situation comedies and in dramas, especially in television feature films, and star roles for women in motion pictures are increasing.)

The major character—the lead character—is the *protagonist*. The protagonist must want something urgently. It is a desperate need—so urgent that to attain his objective becomes a life-and-death matter to him. Now, do not take the term *life and death* literally. It is not a question of kill or be killed unless your script really does revolve around a murder theme. Whatever the protagonist wants urgently is what sets up the problem and the conflict, as well as what spurs the audience to root for him. The audience must want him to achieve his goal.

THE PROTAGONIST'S GOAL

It must not be easy for the protagonist to reach his objective and resolve the problem. Obstacles must be *counterthrust* in his path as the story advances—as the protagonist thrusts ahead in pursuit of the goal. The counterthrusts are provided by the *antagonist*. (Chapter 4 deals with the role of the antagonist.)

First, the protagonist's role needs to be fully explored and understood. A classic contemporary example that illustrates this point in a comedic vein, the protagonist's desperate need (for him, a life-and-death need) to attain an objective, is the motion picture comedy *Silent Movie,* original screenplay by Mel Brooks (who also has the star role as Mel Funn, protagonist).

Mel Funn is desperate for a comeback in the movies after his downfall as a director. Alcohol has wrecked his career. To reestablish himself, he needs to get studio backing from the studio chief (played by Sid Caesar) to make a picture. But what kind of picture? It has to be something different and catchy to lure the film producer into backing it. Funn's two associates (played by Dom DeLuise and Marty Feldman) suggest he make a silent movie. Mel Funn accepts the suggestion. It sounds great. Along with his associates, he drives to the studio on a pink cloud of hope.

The film producer does not share such enthusiasm. He needs a smash hit to save his company from financial disaster. A giant New York film company, Engulf and Devour, is ready to pounce and grab control of his studio by nefarious means.

What's a silent movie? The producer doesn't see popular appeal in a film of this nature. Mel Funn is even more desperate. But one of his associates nudges him and hoarsely whispers that Mel needs to get stars. This is a suggestion the producer accepts. He will back the silent movie if it has stars.

Mel Funn has an objective now—a life-and-death one—a goal made more difficult by his having to sign stars for his picture. This is very clever screenwriting, for not only does this intensify in comedic terms what the protagonist must achieve, but it adds a new dimension to the comedy. Funn's attempts to convince the stars to act in his silent movie provide some superb comedy vignettes. The goal is intensified, and suspense builds as the head of Engulf and Devour counterthrusts to try to stop him.

In *Jaws,* the major goal of protagonist Police Chief Brody is to rid the waters of the killer shark. But first he has another objective—to convince the mayor of the resort beach town that he must close the beaches to protect the public, many of them vacationers and swimmers. The mayor opposes him until the growing number of shark-caused deaths is too much for him to ignore.

Finally he closes the beaches, thus enabling Brody to accomplish his first objective. This opens the way for the major goal—the tremendous and altogether thrill-packed effort to kill the shark (and put Universal's $6,000,000 mechanical shark to work, creating heart-pumping, edge-of-the-seat excitement).

Although the beginning of *Jaws* does not plunge the protagonist into the major goal, the shark strikes immediately at the start of the picture. Its cumulative assaults remain a major part of the story line throughout. Therefore, the audience sees Brody beset by an ever-increasing difficulty in trying to achieve his objective.

Note, too, that in the hair-raising boat ride to hunt and destroy the shark, Brody's objective is shared by the bounty hunter and the oceanographer. But it is Brody who is victor over the shark. He is the protagonist, and the audiences root for him to win. They care about him and not the greed-driven bounty hunter or the oceanographer, who have no real stake in it at all. It is the protagonist, then, who must figure in the resolution and not be outdone or overshadowed by a lesser character.

In *Midnight Express* (based on the true story of Billy Hayes from the Book *Midnight Express* by Billy Hayes and William Hoffer, screenplay by Oliver Stone), Billy desperately wants to get out of the Turkish prison after he is caught and sentenced on a narcotics-smuggling charge. This is his driving aim, intensified when he has to abandon, step by step, any hope of ever gaining his freedom.

But finally, when he is being mercilessly beaten by a prison guard, he packs all his remaining strength—every ounce of defense mechanism that he possesses—into one smashing retaliatory blow, and he escapes. His objective is a strong one and has audiences rooting for him all the way to his joyous hop and skip out the prison gates. The screenplay is an adaptation of a book based on the actual story of Billy's ordeal, and the movie won an Oscar for best picture.

Jack Nicholson stars as the protagonist in *One Flew Over the Cuckoo's Nest* who is placed in a mental institution after his arrest and conviction for a fairly minor crime. It is never determined whether or not he really is a mental case. Although he enters the mental institution, his purpose is to get out of the whole thing.

As soon as he meets his inmate companions, his main objective becomes to liberate these spiritless, joyless people. His objective is established in the screenplay quickly enough to make that the thrust of the story line. When the largest and strongest inmate physically rips a water fountain from the floor, hurls it out the window, and then leaps out himself, the protagonist has attained his objective, because someone has flown out the cuckoo's nest to freedom.

Audiences, too, exult over witnessing this wonderfully dramatic escape. It is joyous to follow on screen his fleeing figure to the very last glimpse, as he seems to blend in with the distant horizon. Drastic punishment is inflicted on the protagonist, but he wins a strong moral victory. He has achieved his objective to liberate the inmates when one flew over the cuckoo's nest.

Another water fountain becomes the focal point of protagonist achievement and magnificent drama in the television feature film *The Autobiography of Miss Jane Pitman,* starring Cicely Tyson. A newspaper reporter interviews a black woman on her one hundredth birthday. He is interested in the life of a black who has a century of living already behind her. In dramatic terms she traces her life from her early days as a slave in the South with a primary objective—to cross the Mississippi. That crossing means she will be free.

Here is presented a protagonist who wins viewer sympathy and wants something with great desperation. In courageous battles against tremendous odds, Jane Pitman achieves her objective. As part of the magnificent performance that won

Tyson an Emmy, she enacts one of the most memorable scenes in television history. In a total accomplishment of her goal, Jane Pitman takes slow, measured, determined steps to the water fountain in the center of town that is reserved exclusively for white people. No black has ever drunk from the fountain. She lowers her mouth to the water spout. From the start of her walk to her drink at the fountain are breathless, marvelous moments.

More Comedy Goals

Jane Pitman presents a strong protagonist with an equally strong goal. Her courage and determination are intrinsic in her characterization. Remember, too, that no matter how comedic a show is, what the protagonist wants is a desperate matter to him.

"Roper's Niece," a "Three's Company" television script written by George Burditt and Paul Wayne, has Jack face a desperate situation. He must keep up his pose as a gay, or Roper, the landlord, will evict him from the apartment that he shares with Chrissy and Janet. Roper offers Jack fifty dollars to date his beautiful niece, Karen. He wants to protect his visiting niece from the sex maniacs and what he considers the other dangerous, disreputable characters of the city, but he knows that his niece will be safe with "gay" Jack.

Needing the fifty dollars, Jack accepts the date and is faced with the problem of keeping his distance from and hands off Karen or having Roper throw him out of the apartment. (Roper, played by Norman Fell, and his wife, played by Audra Lindley, eventually left "Three's Company" for their own spin-off show, "The Ropers," which was later canceled.)

For Jack, the protagonist, having to refrain from any physical contact with the tempting, beautiful Karen is as important an objective with as much desperation attached as possible.

Louie, the brash, runty dispatcher of the television show "Taxi," is desperately faced with the need for his brother, a gambler, to take their mother with him to Las Vegas for her health. Louie is a devoted son, and since the brother's devotion is to his gambling, it plunges Louie into a very desperate situation. How does this segment resolve the problem? It forces the brother, as the loser in a poker game, to take the mother to Las Vegas for two weeks, with the additional features of meals and some shows.

In another episode of "Taxi," cabdriver Alex is robbed by a passenger and shot in the ear. This plunges Alex into a desperate fear for his life and a conflict over whether he should remain a taxi driver. The fear and his conflict build to his quitting his work to become a waiter. Of course, he returns to driving a taxi. The script provides hilarious comedy, but it does not diminish Alex's desperate need to save himself from the dangers of driving a taxi in New York.

Drama, Again

Harry, the police officer played by Clint Eastwood in the motion picture *Dirty Harry,* embarks on a desperate mission to capture a sniper. He is also beset by the heavy criticism of his department superiors for his hardfisted tactics, even to the point of his being suspected of being the killer. As the odds against him compound, his need to attain his objective intensifies.

Serpico tries to fight corruption in the New York City police department. That is his driving goal in the motion picture of that name, taken from the book *Serpico.* In *Brotherhood of the Bell,* a made-for-television film starring Glenn Ford, his role as protagonist sets his driving, intense objective: his need to break out of an Ivy League version of a Mafia-type organization. After futile attempts to convince the police, college, and city officials of the dreadful and criminal happenings, he is succeeding as the drama ends.

MUST THERE ALWAYS BE HAPPY ENDINGS?

Must the objective always be attained by the protagonist? Must there be a happy ending?

Shakespeare's great dramas were all tragedies and have, in a literary sense, remained immortal. That same immortality in quality and depth of the drama is attached to the Greek tragedies. But the audiences expected the tragedies and accepted them as their form of theater fare. Whatever Shakespeare wrote that concluded with a protagonist victory was comedy. There is nothing obligatory today about happy endings except that they are more appealing to motion picture audiences and to the home viewers.

In situation comedies, as in all comedies, the happy ending *is* obligatory. The exception would be a protagonist whose forte would be bungling—in a comedic vein. But usually he, too, through no fault of his own, achieves as part of the friendly bungling what he needs to solve the problem.

In longer-form television shows, moral victories despite tragic endings have been highly effective. Courage displayed in battling a terminal illness has been the theme of several appealing features for television. *Eric,* a television feature written by Carol and Nigel McKeand, tells of Eric's courageous struggle against a terminal illness that gives this fine script an overtone not of sadness, but of hope and strength despite Eric's inevitable death.

The love story of Oliver and Jenny (Ryan O'Neal and Ali McGraw) in *Love Story* ends tragically: Jenny dies. The tragedy does not detract from the appeal of the motion picture, because the story is concerned with love, not illness or death. In fact, Jenny's fatal illness seems contrived because there has not been any foreshadowing or planting of warning clues—not even the most subtle or oblique. (Chapter 8, "Resolution," includes these aspects.) The audiences are charmed by the love story, and by the idea that strong love endures to the end of the film. (Besides, Jenny's death leaves the door open for the sequel, *Oliver's Story.* Although it probably was not preplanned in the writing of *Love Story,* it followed the filmmaking pattern of the runaway success begetting the sequel.)

In an episode of "M*A*S*H," Colonel Henry Blake (as played by McLean Stevenson), a favorite of the men of his company, has received word that he is going to be rotated back to the United States. His objective is the reunion with his wife and daughter. The men want that for him, too. Yet the strong bond between the colonel and his unit makes it difficult for him and his men to say goodbye. Those ambivalent feelings provide the conflict situations that play the serious with the comedy of the show.

Finally, the colonel is leaving. He and his men are shaking hands. But the restrained leave-taking does not hold up. Warm embraces are substituted. The colonel's plane is waiting. He flies away. Later, Radar, who has been close to the colonel, listens to the radio.

A news report breaks into a musical program. The colonel is dead, killed when an enemy plane shot down his aircraft. Here is tragedy in the midst of comedy. It works because of the depth of feeling in the episode's theme. "M*A*S*H" is one of the television comedies not so lightweight that such a tragic turn of events would appear totally disjointed.

Sometimes a fatal accident or illness is arranged on television because of the need to explain to the audience the departure of a major character. The script must be right in keeping with the protagonist's objective, the mood, and consistency in the writing.

ONLY ONE PROTAGONIST

But can there be more than one protagonist? This is a question that can perplex the new writer, and it is essential that this vital ingredient in setting the story line of your script be placed in the right perspective. There can be only *one* protagonist. Even when the division of the activity between two major characters appears to be quite equal, an analysis of the story line will show that one character has the strong lead as protagonist— has the strongest objective and is the driving force.

Oliver and Jenny are in love. There is no doubt that each as fully loves the other. That makes *Love Story*. But Oliver has the greater challenge and need because he marries Jenny over his father's opposition and is therefore cut off from the father's wealth and influence. This compounds Oliver's romantic objective with his need to succeed in his legal career on his own, without his father's help. Jenny shares Oliver's love, but hers is the more passive role.

The passivity is not ascribed to her role because she dies, but because she is not active in thrusting the story forward. In the famous *Camille,* the play that became a much acclaimed motion picture, Camille dies. Greta Garbo, who played Camille on screen, and other stars who followed her in the remakes of the movie, did not select *Camille* as their vehicle for anything less than the strong lead. That Camille dies in the powerful romantic story does not detract from her role as protagonist. Camille is not Jenny. Note, too, that one of the best-remembered lines in *Love Story* (most quoted and also parodied) is the one defining love as "never having to say you're sorry." This is Oliver's line. Indeed, the focus is on him.

What about *Romeo and Juliet?* "Are they not equal protagonists?" you may ask. In this great love tragedy, each has a strong role. They die together, and it is their love for each other that has caused the sequence leading to the deaths of both. It is Juliet who drinks the herbal potion to simulate death—the purpose, to avoid a loveless marriage to Paris that her parents are forcing on her. This is a crucial step that provokes the ultimate tragedy. Romeo, having been banished, returns secretly to her but has failed to receive the explanatory message. Thinking her dead, he kills himself.

But what has really set off the chain of events leading to the tragedy? The primary motivation is the banishment of Romeo. Challenged to a duel by Tybalt, Juliet's cousin, Romeo kills him and is forced to flee the land under threat of imprisonment and death. This sets in motion the subsequent chain of events ending in the tragedy. Thus, in terms of thrusting the story line forward, Juliet's simulation of death to avoid marrying Paris is caused by what has happened to Romeo. It is Romeo who starts the story line in motion when he secretly crashes Juliet's party. It is he who, wandering around the garden, catches sight of Juliet on the balcony. This leads into the famous balcony scene. Later, thinking Juliet dead, he kills himself. Awakening from her simulated death when the potion wears off and seeing her lover dead, she takes her own life.

In the highly acclaimed play *West Side Story,* by Arthur Laurents, and in the motion picture adaptation, the story line is patterned on the Romeo and Juliet premise in a contemporary setting.

Butch Cassidy and the Sundance Kid are outlaw partners. But Butch (Paul Newman) has the stronger role. Historically, he was the leader of the Hole-in-the-Wall Gang, and one of the early scenes of the motion picture also sets him in that lead position. Another of the scenes spotlighting him in this major role is the bike-riding one that also introduces Burt Bacharach's "Raindrops Keep Falling on My Head," the song that became number one on the charts. Butch rides a bike around Etta Place's little house where she is in bed with Sundance. As he circles 'round and 'round, he also clearly expresses his intentions. He wants Etta for himself. She awakens and joins him outside in what, with her on the handlebars, becomes a rollicking ride.

During the bicycle sequence, the delightful "Raindrops Keep Falling on My Head" is sung by B. J. Thomas, recording singer who rose to singing stardom, his popularity and the song's simultaneously building. Certainly, too, this wonderful bike-ride sequence further places Butch as chief protagonist of this Western heist saga. What more can a man want besides a hit song and a woman—except to rob a bank?

Remember: Even though you require two strong leads for the teleplay or motion picture you want to tell and sell, you should have one protagonist only to carry the strongest thrust of the story. On the protagonist is bestowed the larger share of positive qualities. The home viewer or theater audience cannot sustain an equal division of interest in more than one lead character.

Sometimes a television show or motion picture carries one or more subplots. The use of subplots is infrequent and depends on the format of the script. The television show "Eight Is Enough" threads two subplots through every episode, each subordinate to the main story line but each setting a definite protagonist problem—protagonist versus antagonist. The main story line and the two subplots are presented in alternate sequences. But for the solution they merge with the main story line, with the lead character or chief protagonist dominant.

Earthquake is one of the disaster-type motion pictures that contain subplots in addition to the main story line. The heroic chief protagonist role that Charlton Heston plays carries the story strength. But surrounding him are subplots stemming from people in various plights, such as the girl who is trapped and nearly raped by the psychotic National Guard trooper, and the daredevil motorcyclist who is about to execute a Knievel-like feat when the earthquake hits.

The motion picture *Nashville* involves multiple stories, with one stonger than the others. Each of these revolves around country and western music, in that respect following the *Grand Hotel* pattern and, predating that, Arnold Bennett's *Imperial Hotel*.

Sometimes the format for these backgrounds of one central area is the use of single episodes, each independent and complete in itself, such as in the television shows "Love Boat," (which contains three or four complete episodes enacted on a cruise ship) and "Fantasy Island" (in which two complete stories in two separate episodes concern the acting out of a fantasy wish by a guest on the island). *California Suite* and *Plaza Suite,* both by Neil Simon, each utilize the basic hotel setting for multiple stories. "Love, American Style," a popular, long-running television show still in syndication, attaches short episodes, many no more than blackouts complete in themselves, to one base—love.

The one factor all these episodes have in common, whether separate segments or subplots, is a protagonist who wants something. His need, whether dramatic or comedic, is urgent and vital to him, and he faces opposition (to be discussed in the following chapter) which provides stumbling blocks in his attempt to achieve his goal. Remember, then: Because the protagonist is of vital importance in wanting something urgently, the viewer must care about the protagonist and want him to succeed in attaining his objective.

QUALITIES OF THE PROTAGONIST

That means the protagonist must possess qualities that are admirable and acceptable to the viewer. The protagonist's traits must have appeal. One false move by the protagonist or the display of a mean trait will cost audience sympathy. Let the protagonist help an old lady cross the street—if it fits naturally into the script—and the viewer will approve the kindness. But if he responds to an appeal for help in a cruel or indifferent way, the viewer will be turned off and will turn *him* off.

Rocky—the loser—wins immediate audience sympathy. He is challenged to fight the champion for the boxing title, and it inspires him to want to succeed. The audience wants that success for him, too. Everyone is rooting for Rocky. Audiences like him for such character traits as his candor, simplicity, capacity to accept the challenge and try for success, and the basic fact that he is the underdog. In his marvelous portrayals of the pathetic underdog against tremendous odds, Charlie Chaplin won screen immortality.

Audiences root for the success of Police Chief Brody over the mayor in wanting the beaches closed because of the menace of the shark, and then in hunting down and killing the shark. Brody is forthright, sincere, and courageous. When he first opposes the mayor, he may be risking his job. But he fights for what he believes in, at whatever the personal cost to him.

These protagonists are acceptable to audiences not only for traits that audiences like, but also because they have a certain morality and ethical sense. They are honest. They have broken no laws. But what of the protagonists who operate outside the law? What about *Butch Cassidy and the Sundance Kid* and other examples of stories whose main characters, although operating unlawfully, are wonderfully appealing to the audiences? This type of protagonist is the antihero, the protagonist who is on the wrong side of the law.

The Antihero Protagonist

The antihero protagonist became a popular screen figure in the sixties, when social protest generated strong antiestablishment feelings. The Vietnam War, the assassinations, and the battle for civil rights were some of the issues that turned public sentiment away from the social order. That decade did not produce halcyon days, nor did dissatisfaction and unrest vanish in the seventies. On the contrary, the shock of Watergate generated new distrust of government and "The Establishment," and so continued the popularity and acceptance of the antihero on the screen.

Let's look at some of these antiheroes. Sonny, played by Al

Pacino, is the protagonist of the motion picture *Dog Day Afternoon,* written by Frank Pierson. Sonny is antihero. His objective in this comedy-drama is to rob a bank. But he is far more successful at endearing himself to audiences. He is amiable, likable, and shows consideration for his hostages—a nice feeling for people.

When, upon his demand, a woman hostage opens the safe and it is empty, she bursts into sobs because the money was picked up that afternoon. She is afraid Sonny will shoot her because the money is not there for him to steal. But Sonny has no intention of killing her. He is surprised that she would expect such a ruthless action from him. It is not her fault, he assures her, that there is no money in the safe. His good traits are showing. He is a likable, humane fellow, not a cold-blooded killer.

He is considerate: He permits his hostages to go to the washroom, taking turns, and he also lets a young woman hostage talk to her husband on the phone to advise him about the care and feeding of their baby in her absence. Nor does he overlook the fact that people, including himself, get hungry. He sends out for pizzas for everyone and generously pays the bill with marked bank money. He has a sense of humor, too.

'But Sonny also has his shrewd side. He is not a dunce. Before he reaches into a cash drawer for bank money, he deactivates an automatic alarm. His sharp eye spots the alarm; he had once worked in a bank and thus knows his way around. He is also able to discern decoy money. Audiences can respect him.

They also understand his motivation in wanting to rob a bank. He needs money to support his wife and children. Why doesn't he get a job? He has a logical and simple answer for that. It's a chicken-and-the-egg puzzler. He cannot work because he doesn't belong to a union, but to join a union, he would first have to get the job. If he worked at a nonunion job, he would be underpaid.

Then, as if this were not enough, he offers even further motivation for having to rob a bank. He needs to get his hands on a substantial sum of money to pay for the sex-change operation of his lover, Leon. (The introduction of Leon, it is noted, occurs far along in the motion picture as one of the story line twists and turns. Chapter 7, "The Build," analyzes *Dog Day Afternoon* in more detail.)

Sonny also wins supporters among the crowd of people who gather in front of the bank in the midst of the excitement. The motion picture is based on an actual bank robbery, and the excellent screenplay reflects the approval and admiration the robber won from the crowd. People cheer Sonny every time he steps outside the bank in the course of negotiations for the release of the hostages. One wave of his hand—one gesture their way—and they roar their approval. Sonny has won his spurs as an antihero who operates outside the Establishment—far out.

Another protagonist in the antihero category (literally, anti-heroine) is the young wife (played by Goldie Hawn) who, in the movie *Sugarland Express*, helps her young husband escape from jail. Compounding the escape, they steal a car for their getaway and force a police officer at gunpoint to drive the car. Despite her unlawful acts, the wife wins quick audience sympathy because she has strong motivation for arranging her husband's jailbreak.

He wants to know why she has set up his escape. Her explanation is warmly understandable to him and to the audience. While he was in jail, she tells him, Welfare took their baby from her and gave the tot to another family. She wants to get the baby back. The audience fervently hopes that she and her husband will successfully elude the police, who are now in pursuit of them, and retrieve their child. This is protagonist antihero activity that gains strong support. Let this appealing young mother get back her baby—Godspeed!

Antihero Butch Cassidy as portrayed in *Butch Cassidy and the Sundance Kid* is an appealing outlaw, and so is partner Sundance. They are charming outlaws with a rich sense of humor.

Another antihero protagonist is Willard, in the motion picture of the same name. What makes him a most unique protagonist is that he acquires a pack of rats as friends. Now generally, rats are repulsive creatures both in reality and on the screen, where they are caught by cameras in sewers, prison cells, and dark cellars when the script calls for such dismal surroundings. But Willard is desperate over his harassment from his mother and his boss. He has a desperate need: to free himself.

To aid him in his drive toward self-liberation are the rats. He makes friends with one he finds loitering in his backyard. News travels fast in the rodent world, and soon Willard's little rat pal is joined by others, until Willard has gathered to himself a large rat pack. They are his subjects. He commands and they obey. Under his orders they destroy his nagging mother and his exploiting, slave-driving boss. What is exceptional about this picture is that audience sympathies are with Willard and his rats. The skillful writing has made him a nice, clean-cut young man overburdened by a nagging mother and a nasty boss. As a sympathetic character he is every bit the protagonist—of the antihero kind.

However, contrary to the rule of thumb that an unpleasing character trait will cause an audience to desert their hero, Willard does display what can be considered a mean or cowardly side of his nature. This occus near the end of the movie. Willard deserts his rodent friends, dooming them. For moral and sanitation reasons it may have been considered wiser to get rid of the rats rather than leave one thousand of the creatures roaming free in a city. But over any moral purpose that may have been considered in making the film, a practical consideration was the preparation of the film for a sequel.

Little Ben is the one rodent survivor of the pack. Audience sympathies switch to Ben, on whom the camera focuses in a close shot, and all his wistfulness. Willard has deserted little Ben, too. But Ben is alive, alone in a desperate situation, but preserved to star in the sequel, the title of which honors him by bearing his name.

Ben also became the subject of the song of that title, sung with ingratiating charm by the boy whose friendship the little rat won. *Willard* illustrates that skillful writing can make a sympathetic protagonist, antihero type, even out of a young man who has command of a killer rat pack. It also shows that rats can also be a sympathetic lot when they are aiding an antihero audiences understand and like.

Archie Bunker (Carroll O'Connor in the role) has long been an antihero as the series star of "All in the Family." Now that Jean Stapleton (Edith) has left the show, he is star of the revised version, "Archie Bunker's Place," which centers around Archie's bar. Archie is a bigot. He is also cheap, penny-pinching, and not opposed to a little larceny if it can put a few extra dollars in his pocket.

In an "All in the Family" segment, Edith loses her locket. She assures Archie that it is not a costly heirloom. Its real value for her is sentimental, for it is a prized gift from her grandmother. Here is where the petty larcenist nature in Archie takes over. He places a higher monetary value on the locket in order to collect insurance for its loss. When the insurance company agent denies his claim because his insurance policy covers only theft, Archie meets that complication by claiming that the locket was stolen.

The show has never allowed Archie to win in the pursuit of larceny, or in his practice of bigotry. The police do catch the thief who did steal the locket, and Edith recovers her piece of jewelry. Archie swallows his defeat and even turns it into personal victory by misinterpreting the incident. Archie's bigotry and larcenous nature always generate laughter. The reasons he gives for these adverse traits are so grossly exaggerated that they point up the ridiculousness of his stance.

Archie expresses other opinions that are not in step with the times, such as his anti–women's liberation views. In the second episode of "Archie Bunker's Place," Jean Stapleton makes a guest appearance as Edith, even though she has left the show. That she has been working on a job accounts for her absence in the skillfully written script. Typical of Archie, he opposes Edith's working on a job and emphasizes, in his way, that a woman's place is in the home looking after her family. His business partner, played by Martin Balsam, is broad-minded, modern, and liberal in his views. Establishing good rapport with Edith, he encourages her to interview for another job about which she is now hesitant. Once again, Archie is defeated in trying to enforce another of his narrow-minded points of view.

Another type of antihero is the Godfather of the novel of that name by Mario Puzo, adapted into a motion picture by Francis

Ford Coppola. Both the novel and motion picture have met with phenomenal success. But the Godfather is no model of ethics and morality. He is head of the Family, a powerful syndicate in control of organized crime. Then how does it happen? How can such a character—head of a mob operating well outside the law—be antihero? The crime syndicate has always been the target of federal agents and other authorities, for example, "The FBI" television series.

It happens because Puzo set out to tell the Godfather's story in personal, human terms. The Godfather's relationship with the Family (members of his syndicate) and his personal relationship with his own family forge an empathetic bond between the Godfather and the motion picture audience and, prior to the film, with the vast number of readers of the blockbuster book. The Godfather wins strong audience sympathy as a compassionate, fair-minded man who is loyal to his people and expects the same measure of loyalty in return.

The motion picture opens with his daughter's wedding. While the wedding reception takes place outdoors, complete with feast and dancing, the Godfather is in the house, holding personal court in his study. He hears out the people who call on him with their problems. To his proven friends he is ready to do favors. But he rejects the desperate plea for financial help from one who had shown disloyalty to him. Audiences cannot fault him for that. He has deep concern for his two sons, Mike and Sonny, and for his daughter. He is not enmeshed in problems about his wife because, typical of Italian women of past generations, she takes care of the household and does that well. But his concern for his children also extends to a young man, Johnnie, a singer who has been rejected for the star role he badly wants in a motion picture. The producer has shut him out. Can Godfather do something?

The Godfather promises Johnnie he'll take care of the matter. When the proposal for Johnnie to be cast in the star role still receives producer rejection, Godfather takes stronger steps. The producer's prize possession is a racehorse. That Godfather intends to keep his promise to Johnnie soon becomes evident, with a present being made to the producer of the severed head of his precious racehorse. Johnnie gets the star part. Godfather is a man of his word in keeping with his own code of honor.

An additional positive quality is his moral sense. He refuses the offer of a rival mob chief to join forces for even more profit than his own syndicate operations yield. The offer is a partnership in the rival syndicate's drug racket and Godfather rejects the offer on moral grounds. Drugs destroy the lives of young people who make up a large proportion of the drug buyers, and he does not want to make narcotics available to them. His rejection of the offer invites retaliation. He is shot. Audience sympathy for him and his family is strengthened all the more because, in his antihero role, he leads the "good" side as opposed to the rival mob that traffics in the drugs that he considers the worst evil of all.

Remember: Through skillful writing you can build as much audience sympathy for an antihero protagonist as for the "straight" hero. Mario Puzo set out to tell a powerful story about the inner workings of an organized crime Family headed by a Godfather and to tell it with sympathy for his antihero. Puzo did not set out to tell a cops-and-robbers type of story of earlier years with a law enforcer such as Melvin Purvis in pursuit of a crime organization and its leader. That is a tale told over and over, on "The FBI" television series and in 1,001 other movies and books. From a different—the reverse—point of view, *The Godfather* succeeds admirably.

Bonnie and Clyde is another successful antihero motion picture. Bonnie and Clyde engage in a crime spree of devastating proportions, and yet they are appealing characters who command strong audience sympathy. Although the two share the action, Clyde (played by Warren Beatty) is the protagonist antihero. He is the leader in planning and carrying out the robberies that result in shoot-outs as the pair attempt to escape during their various capers. It is Clyde, too, who prevails on Bonnie (played by Faye Dunaway) to embark on a life of crime with him. They are an appealing pair with a sense of humor, and they hold audiences to them in an empathetic bond. Again, this is the reverse of the typical cops-and-robbers approach, and with the freshly appealing quality of its lead characters, it was developed into a highly successful film.

Another antihero protagonist is played by Steve McQueen in

the motion picture *The Getaway.* He enlists his wife—Ali McGraw in the role—to get him out of jail through her favors to the warden. He has a big caper planned, which he and his partners carry out as soon as he obtains his freedom. But his partners turn out to be the real villains as they attempt to thwart him in plot twists that involve cross and double cross. It is the antihero protagonist with whom the audiences are in sympathy—with him and his wife—and they root for him to recover his share of the loot out of which he has been double-crossed.

Once in a while a protagonist antihero is created whose sole appeal to the audience is fascination. Such a fascinating character is Regina of *The Little Foxes,* the notable play by Lillian Hellman that later was adapted into an equally fine screenplay. Regina is a thoroughly fascinating character, ruthless in her pursuit of her objective and without regard for who may get hurt as she drives toward her goal. Her big ambition is to get out of the town and the home in which she feels a bondage and go to Chicago. But she wants to settle there in style as a rich woman. To achieve her goal she must overcome such obstacles as a sick husband from whom she has been separated for some years. She accomplishes her ruthless purpose by causing his death. When he is stricken by a heart attack and cannot reach for his medicine, she refuses to get it for him. She is one step closer to her objective. After she completes her dealings with her brothers—particularly the greedy Ben, a man she outmatches in ruthlessness—she is ready to take the train in high style to Chicago.

Indeed, she is fascinating. Although she is devoid of admirable personal traits with which other antiheroes are endowed, her strong self-will, her brittle tongue and sharp wit, and her beauty (required of the stars who have portrayed Regina) combine to captivate audiences on stage and screen and will likely continue to do so whenever *The Little Foxes* is enacted on the boards or on film. Tallulah Bankhead, the original star of *The Little Foxes,* enhanced the fascination of a superbly drawn character with a remarkable performance. But it is the character as created by Hellman that has the inherent fascination.

More popularly known to the public is the fascinating Scarlett O'Hara, portrayed on screen by Vivien Leigh in the remarkable film *Gone with the Wind*. She has spirit—an intense, driving force within her that enables her to face, during the Civil War, the destruction of the society of the South that she had known and into which she had been born.

She has enough spirit and strength of character to ride out of an Atlanta in flames, and she also helps others escape the city of raging fires. On the weaker and less moral side, she is obsessed with love for Ashley (or at least a romantic fantasy about him), and with that as her primary romantic interest, she manipulates other men who want her, marrying without love, and then as a widow, weds Rhett Butler in a marriage of convenience. Audiences are more sympathetic with Rhett than Scarlett when their little girl suffers a fatal accident and applaud him when he walks out on her. His walkout occurs at the moment that she finally wants him.

Yet she is still the Scarlett O'Hara propelled by her own self-interest. Her need for Rhett is not born of a newly awakened love for him, but of her realization that Ashley does not love her and never did. Just the same, she is fascinating, and because she is such a fascinating character, she commands interest from the first to the last sight of her on screen. After Atlanta burns to the ground, she becomes determined to reach her family plantation. There is no doubt that Scarlett O'Hara will get there.

A word can be said about the memorable performances. David Selznick conducted an extensive search for the right actress to play Scarlett O'Hara. The fascination of the character needed to project on screen. Although unknowns were considered for the part, none was found to be right for this extraordinary role.

Clark Gable as Rhett Butler is unforgettable, too. So are Ashley and Melanie, portrayed by Leslie Howard and Olivia de Havilland. But the character of Scarlett O'Hara is the trademark of the movie. It is not an easy character for the writer to create. Such a portrayal, depending on the fascination of the character, is a difficult challenge for the writer. If this is the type of protagonist you select, remember that you are relying on the fascination of your character—and solely that—to win and hold audience interest. This is the challenge.

Basically, whatever kind of protagonist you choose for your leading character, the urgent need for the protagonist to fulfill an objective must be established. This includes establishing an empathetic bond between the viewer and your protagonist. Even the fascinating protagonist who wins no sympathy for well-intended motivations will have the audience fascinated enough to hope for the protagonist's achievement of the objective sought.

TIME DEADLINE

The following hint for intensifying the urgency of the protagonist's need to obtain a goal does not apply to every type of story. But here is the suggestion if it has a natural place in your story and will not be contrived: Whether the script is drama, melodrama, mystery, adventure, or comedy, a deadline of a given time will heighten the urgency. The deadline for needing to achieve a goal has a life-and-death connotation and thus carries built-in suspense.

A classic example is the motion picture *High Noon,* with Gary Cooper starring as the sheriff of a western town. Three gunmen are expected to ride into town at high noon to kill the sheriff. As the deadline for death draws nearer, the fear of the townspeople grows. No one wants to be caught in the midst of gunfire. They desert the sheriff. He stands alone—the lone man on the main street—when the gunmen ride into town.

Zero hour is exactly high noon. The noon deadline has served to add tension throughout the film. The big town clock relentlessly ticks away the hours and minutes to the fateful time. Close shots of the big clock, reminding the audience at well-paced intervals of the life-and-death deadline, are effective in heightening the suspense.

A story has made industry rounds that *High Noon* was previewed before its general release and that the motion picture was not well received. But someone came up with a bright idea about what the picture lacked. As the story goes, it was a producer's wife who said, "It needs clocks." One cannot vouch for the validity of the story. But if *High Noon* at first did not have the high noon deadline, it would surely have lacked the cohesiveness and tension that the life-and-death timing give it. A deadline cannot and should not be forced or contrived, but where it can logically and naturally fit, it can be a decided asset.

In *Murder on the Orient Express,* Hercule Poirot has set himself the deadline of solving the murder before the Orient Express reaches its destination. A snowstorm stalls the train at the time the murder is committed and during the investigation, but a crew works through the night to clear the tracks. There are several intercuts to the workmen digging to free the train from its snow trap. These shots of the excavation efforts point out the crucial passage of time to the deadline. This technique adds further suspense to that created by the murder aboard the train and the situation of a murderer being one of the passengers.

There are many other variations of the life-and-death situation in graphic time terms. One is the police detective out of favor with the chief, given forty-eight hours to prove correct his theory of the crime's solution—in other words, solve the crime or be demoted to walking a beat. Another example is the need for a doctor or a key police officer to find the unwitting carrier of a dread, rare disease in six hours, the deadline time before which an entire population will otherwise be infected. *Panic in the Streets,* an original screenplay of the 1940s and an Oscar winner, was one of the first—possibly *the* first—of the films that build around this deadline theme. In that film, bubonic plague was the dread disease that caused the intensive manhunt deadline.

The theme is still a popular one, particularly on television shows. But life-and-death deadlines do not apply only to suspense-crime scripts. Many a comedy gives the protagonist a deadline, too.

If you can inject a deadline into your story without having it appear contrived, it can strengthen the building of suspense. But all-important is the protagonist who holds viewer interest. Give your protagonist a pressing need to fulfill an objective, and the character traits and credible motivation to establish audience empathy, and your screenplay or teleplay will contain some primary ingredients to form a base from which to launch your work.

However, another primary character is also essential: the antagonist. The antagonist provides the obstacles in the path of the protagonist—the conflicts or crosscurrents which provide the suspense and a "What will happen next?" excitement. Let's take a look at the antagonist—the all-important counterforce.

4

The Antagonist as Counterthrust

The famous line in the motion picture *Star Wars,* now a part of our popular culture, constitutes a prayer. Offering the hope that the Force be with the heroic protagonist and his allies is tantamount to saying "May God be with you." Luke Skywalker, the heroic, hard-pressed protagonist, urgently wants what becomes a multiple objective:

1. He sets out to save his own life by escaping the evil Imperial storm troopers so he can join the Rebel forces, and in so doing, also find out what happened to his father, whom he fears met a tragic fate.

2. This mission intensifies into the desperate need to rescue the princess, who has been kidnapped by the Imperial oppressors.

3. Luke wants to help defeat the Imperial oppressors, who seek to enslave the galaxy. They are formidable foes who might crush the hero, for the odds are on their side. Luke's desire to help overthrow the Empire and reestablish the Republic includes a dangerous attempt to rescue the princess, who is one of the Rebel leaders. The defeat of the Empire and the rescue of the princess combine to become the primary or most urgent objective.

The overpoweringly evil leader of the merciless enemy is Darth Vader, Lord of the Dark Sith. This sinister character, who is now a legend of our time (no Halloween party is complete without several guests in Darth Vader costumes), is the *antagonist*—the archvillain.

He and his space storm troopers *block* every advancement of the protagonist and his allies. The *antagonist* and the forces he leads supply the *counterthrust* against the *protagonist thrusting ahead* in the attempts to achieve the objective. These *counterthrusts* provide the conflict and so the suspense, causing the audience to ask whether the hero protagonist and his Rebel allies will succeed.

Will the princess be rescued? Will the Death Star, a monumentally huge engine of death capable of destroying entire planets, be defeated and destroyed? The momentum builds, climaxing in a thrill-packed space battle to demolish the enemy while the enemy piles on the counterthrusts.

THRUST AND COUNTERTHRUST

The basic pattern of *Star Wars* follows the formula of the Western's "good guys versus bad guys." Whether on the ranch, on the trail, or in outer space, the pattern of protagonist versus antagonist is clear-cut. Keep in mind that a protagonist should not move forward in screenplay or teleplay of any type without the antagonist counterthrusting these advances step by step, which requires the protagonist to make a new move to circumvent the opposition. In turn, the antagonist again counterthrusts, with the cross-purpose pattern continuing the conflict in progressively rising action. The protagonist advances, then the antagonist counterthrusts, creating this pattern:

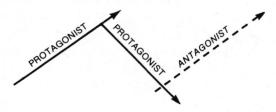

FIGURE 4-1. Protagonist drops back at antagonist's counterthrust. Then protagonist advance sets back antagonist, etc.

When the protagonist acts again, the antagonist will reply with a new cross-purpose or counterthrust.

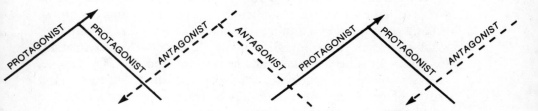

FIGURE 4–2.

These encounters create and sustain interest. Every forward thrust of the protagonist should give this chief character, as well as the audience, new hope of protagonist success. Every setback then creates new suspense. Will he make it? Will he succeed? It is the injection of the antagonist role that produces this suspense. If the protagonist kept on advancing without opposition, there would be no conflict, no suspense, and no story.

ANTAGONISTS—INSIDE AND OUTSIDE THE LAW

Now, what is the composition of the antagonist? Just as there are many variations on the type of protagonist, antagonists come in all shapes and sizes. Just as the protagonist objectives require believable motivation, the antagonist must have credible motivation for blocking the way. Why does he want to stop the protagonist? Sometimes the antagonist is psychotic, especially if perpetrating a series of murders, but even the psychotic character carries with him some basis for his irrationality.

In back of many a crime plaguing McGarrett on "Hawaii Five-O" is the cunning antagonist Wo-Fat. Not only is this sinister villain a formidable match for McGarrett, but he has always been permitted to escape at the end of each episode in which he is featured as the foe, so that he can return with another diabolical scheme for McGarrett to crush. Such is the popularity of some of the most rascally of antagonists. But finally, Wo-Fat has been permitted to be killed off, only because "Hawaii Five-O" has ended its long run on CBS television.

Wo-Fat was terminated in the final episode, but he made his

diabolical mark as a television antagonist. Create an outstanding antagonist, and you, too, can make your mark on a series show of the detective-suspense genre. Such a formidable antagonist serves all the more as a challenge to the protagonist, who, in besting the especially cunning foe, shows to his finest advantage.

Of all the devilish antagonists that Sherlock Holmes brought to boot, Moriarty ranked at the top of the list. Of course, Holmes solved the crimes this villain perpetrated, but the Conan Doyle of nearly a century ago allowed him to escape so that he could be brought back to perpetrate still another crime.

Moriarty still lives. Nicholas Meyer's stunning Sherlockian first novel, *The Seven-Per-Cent Solution,* and then the screenplay adapted by him from his book, pitted Holmes against Moriarty. Whenever another screenplay centered on Holmes reaches the screen, odds are that the archvillain is Moriarty.

Bob Kane, who created Batman as a comic book hero for Detective Comics (DC), pitted the great caped figure against the Penguin as well as a wide assortment of other ingenious criminals with their own special trademarks. Of course, Batman has always outwitted the Penguin, but neither on comic book pages or in television episodes has the Penguin ever been permanently retired.

One of the most memorable archvillains of all time was the Fat Man of Dashiell Hammett's *The Maltese Falcon,* adapted into the screenplay of that name. *The Maltese Falcon* film, premiering in the 1940s, still reappears on television on late shows or the late, late show. Humphrey Bogart starred as Sam Spade, the private eye, with the famous Bogart gravelly voice and tough manner giving a special distinction to Sam Spade that well lived up to the special qualities of this detective originally created on the printed page. Conversely, Sydney Greenstreet, very obese himself, immortalized the antagonist character known as the Fat Man. The courteous manner, his literate speech combined with a soft but sinister chuckle, and his enormous size won him great success as the archvillain—not only in *The Maltese Falcon* but also in movies to follow in which he was similarly cast.

Another popular antagonist of that decade was Peter Lorre of the wide pop eyes and lisp, who in *The Maltese Falcon* was one of the coconspirators. In sharp contrast to Greenstreet, he was a small, short man, but that gave him all the more distinction as an ally of the archvillain or in other films when Lorre himself played the antagonist supervillain. His, too, became a magic name in thriller movies, and it was not unusual for him to be cast as the superantagonist, performing solo in that role.

However, it must be pointed out that although the Greenstreet and Lorre names had big drawing power—audiences anticipated that a suspense-thriller with either of them as archvillain would have to be good—the real measuring rod for the successful motion picture or teleplay is the writing. It is the author who creates the character portrayals. Greenstreet could not have become renowned as the Fat Man antagonist of *The Maltese Falcon* if the characterization had not already been set in the writing. Conversely, Humphrey Bogart molded the Sam Spade role. But first, the rich characterization had to be written.

Keep in mind, too, that just as there can be only one protagonist, only one antagonist can enact the major role of opposition. The protagonist can have an ally or allies, but he must be the driving force who has the urgent need to attain an objective. Similarly, the antagonist can have supporters in the nasty business of placing obstacles in the protagonist's path, but one antagonist takes the lead.

In *Dog Day Afternoon,* a large contingent of police are trying to capture Sonny and his partner Sal, who hold hostages in the bank that they rob. As pointed out earlier, Sonny is the antihero protagonist. This is his story. Of the opposition, although police surround the bank and police sharpshooters are posted on rooftops of the bank and surrounding buildings, the leader of the antagonist force is Police Detective Moretti. He gives the orders and sets up traps for Sonny, even though in the line of command the commissioner is above him. He is the moving antagonist force—the leader.

A posse hunts Butch Cassidy and Sundance, with the leader directing them. He is chief antagonist, directing his posse in trying to track down the outlaws. *Sugarland Express* has the police as opposition to the young wife who wants to recover her baby, with her husband her ally. The fact that the couple forces, at gunpoint, a policeman to drive the car stolen for their getaway heightens the opposition of the law enforcement officers.

But the antihero protagonist operating outside the law does not necessarily have a lawman antagonist as opposition. The type of antagonist depends upon the story. In the motion picture *The Getaway,* the antihero protagonist is a partner in a caper after he is released from jail. The stakes are high. The caper is successful. But the antagonist is not the law officer in pursuit of the antihero outside the law. Forced to shoot a double-crossing partner who recovered his share of the loot, the protagonist is set upon by the other partners in the big caper. Of these villains—and they are a mean lot—the warden is the leader, the archantagonist. Happily for the antihero, he is ready for the ambush set up for him; in a shoot-out he kills them all.

Now, note that the antihero protagonist and the antagonist and his forces are all operating outside the law. They have been partners in crime. But what separates the protagonist from his partners in the antagonist ranks is that the antihero is just that—the hero to the audience though engaged in an illicit caper. The heavies—the lead antagonist and his allies—are ruthless. They are devoid of conscience and compassion, qualities which the antihero possesses. That sets them apart as the evildoers, in contrast to the likable antihero, even though they were partners in pulling the caper. Remember that the meaner the heavy—and his allies if he leads a group or mob—and the more ruthless and craftier he is, the greater the challenge the protagonist faces, and each of the more challenging counterthrusts serves to heighten suspense.

Another group or gang type of opposition, with the leader giving the orders as the prime antagonist, appears in the motion picture *Oklahoma Crude.* The syndicate leader/spokesman besets the woman owner, played by Faye Dunaway, who believes that the oil well she inherited from her father will prove a gusher. When she defies the syndicate demand that she sell out to them, the leader antagonist and his men intensify their threats against her to the point of attempting to burn her out.

However, notice that the $350,000 sale price for this original screenplay was no doubt for more than a plot concerning a beautiful woman protagonist against a syndicate and its leader. A man wanders her way seeking a job and also offering to help her in fighting the syndicate. He establishes the secondary conflict because she hates men and thinks she can handle the problem herself. She doesn't need him. But he sticks around, and the fact that this gritty male is portrayed by George C. Scott makes the conflict a highly entertaining one. Eventually, she becomes romantically involved with him, and they join forces in defeating the foe in the final violent attempt to force her hand.

Note: The woman-man conflict is part of the development of the screenplay—part of the build (as discussed in Chapter 7). It greatly enhances the film. The man who tries and finally succeeds in wearing down her man-hating attitude is not the antagonist of the plot line. The syndicate leader/spokesman with his mob represents the prime antagonist set on forcing the oil well sale. But again, keep in mind what ingenious screenwriting can do by providing the woman protagonist with a man-hating attitude trait and so bestowing on the script the quite delightful woman-man conflict that gave *Oklahoma Crude* its "plus" value—in terms of dollars, too.

A chief antagonist surrounded by a group of supporters is not limited to crime dramas. This alignment can be found in any type of script, depending on the story being told. For example, on the light side is the comedy *Silent Movie,* written by and starring Mel Brooks. The chief antagonist, played by Harry Gould, is the head of the firm of Engulf and Devour, intent on preventing Mel Funn (Brooks) from making his silent movie with stars, which represents his one big chance of making a comeback in the film industry. The Engulf and Devour chief, with his board of directors (his group) in total agreement, misses no twist and turn in his devious efforts to thwart Mel Funn, even to the point of engineering the theft of the film as the picture is about to be premiered.

An antagonist who is outstanding in a motion picture is Nurse Ratched of *One Flew Over the Cuckoo's Nest.* The mental institution serves as a natural enemy of its inmates. Yet the attendants of this institution are like faceless robots acting under orders, and the orders are given by Nurse Ratched. She is a remarkably effective antagonist through a quiet malevolence.

She doesn't need to rampage or rage to enforce her highly repressive measures. In moments of triumph her tight, exultant smile says it all. Louise Fletcher as Nurse Ratched gives an award-winning performance. She is fine, but the writing had to be the basis for her interpretation.

Every time McMurphy (Jack Nicholson) advances a step in his intention of liberating the sorrowful inmates, she strikes back. She refuses to allow McMurphy to tune in the World Series for all of them. McMurphy works hard to persuade her to allow a vote. These sad sacks do not produce enough votes.

The next day a second vote is taken. The count is improved, but stills falls one short of a majority. McMurphy exerts his energies and persuasive powers to muster up that one vote. The voting takes place during a group therapy session. By the time the vote is cast that wins a majority for the World Series, Ratched ends the session and so the vote is not counted in.

The camera picks up in close shot her exultant expression, and it is powerful in its counterpurpose. The cross-purpose conflicts of protagonist versus antagonist are strongly written into the script, which was adapted by Lawrence Hauben and Bo Goldman from Ken Kesey's novel of that name. Louise Fletcher makes the antagonist role all the more unforgettable by her performance.

The conflict is strong as she counterthrusts every advance step McMurphy makes. The Nurse Ratched role is a striking, clear-cut example of the antagonist working to defeat the protagonist. It points up the strength of a script by the strength of the opposition—the antagonist in cross-purpose conflict against the protagonist.

In *North Dallas Forty,* the owner of the commercial football team is the primary antagonist. He is crass, ruthless, and inhumane in his treatment of his players, especially Paul, the protagonist played by Nick Nolte. Paul is devoted to playing football, although he suffers the aches and bruises that are part of the professional football package—and he suffers the abuse of both owner and coach.

The team's owner is the major foe—the major antagonist. He has support from the coach, who enjoys deflating Paul. But it is the owner who delivers the final blow against Paul. Just as the protagonist must be the driving force in motion picture or teleplay and so finally determines the outcome, the antagonist—the major foe—stands out above any allies in dealing the protagonist what he hopes will be a crushing blow. The owner delivers that cruncher: He refuses to let Paul play in the big game. But Paul achieves a moral victory. He is able to pick up and quit the game.

McMurphy's victory in *One Flew Over the Cuckoo's Nest* is achieved, too, when the big Indian smashes the window by flinging the fountain through it and escapes. These triumphs are all the more strengthened by the antagonist, who is crafty enough and mean enough to provide those obstacles that give the protagonist such a difficult time.

THE LIKABLE ANTAGONIST

Another type of antagonist may be personable and project definite audience appeal while acting as a counterforce to the protagonist. An antagonist of this type often is featured in romantic comedies in which the man-woman relationship theme develops in conflict. *The Goodbye Girl,* by Neil Simon, has as protagonist Pamela (played by Marsha Mason), who has a relationship problem with men. They leave her. The latest to exit from her life with nothing more than a farewell note was her lover Tony, an actor who left New York—the locale for *The Goodbye Girl*—for Hollywood.

In making this move, he rents the apartment he shared with Pamela and for which he holds the lease, to a new tenant, Eliot, played by Richard Dreyfuss. Eliot becomes the instant antagonist, the first conflict with Pamela being his demand that she move out of the apartment with her little girl. A truce is effected, but only in the matter of her and the child being allowed to share the apartment with him. The conflict between them continues to build. However, an attraction for one another also builds into what appears to be love. Then it happens to her—the shattering moment. He, too, is leaving, called to Hollywood on an acting assignment.

Again, in script terms, his role as antagonist sharpens. Once again, Pamela lives up to the title of the move as the girl to whom men say goodbye. However, the goodbye pattern is breaking—almost. He wants her to go out to Hollywood with him, but she refuses. The trek out there is not for her and her little girl. But love has really taken root. What sheer joyousness she feels and expresses at the moment before he drives away in the taxi! He will be back.

Interest is sustained through the conflict of the relationship—the cross-purposes of protagonist Pamela and Eliot. An antagonist need not have a gun in hand or carry around a headful of Machiavellian schemes. Emotional and romantic conflicts can also line up protagonist and antagonist against one another. But one factor must be considered. In a two-character conflict relationship that will eventually build to love, the likability of the antagonist must be established even though he and the protagonist are at sword's point a good part of their battling way. No one wants to see the protagonist eventually fall in love with the antagonist if he is portrayed as unpleasant and unattractive.

Of course, the wife who starts out being in love with her husband, only to discover that he is a criminal, is opposed by an antagonist who is not intended as anything but a diabolical character for whom, usually, a police investigator is setting a trap.

The motion picture *Gaslight,* adapted from the play by that name, stars Ingrid Bergman and Charles Boyer, with Boyer as antagonist, the criminal who is trying to drive his wife crazy. The "gaslight effect," the lights going dim, is part of this trickery. In a memorable, climactic scene in which the wife has become fully aware of her husband's evil intent, she angrily and mockingly turns on him. Even though at the start of *Gaslight* she has no idea of his criminal purpose, the show builds to the audience suspicion of his nefarious doings and the ultimate wish for his exposure.

The Two Mrs. Carrolls, a motion picture adapted from the play, involves the loving wife protagonist whose growing suspicions that her husband is a murderer leads to the inevitable terrifying scene in which he attempts also to kill her.

Once in a while, the husband who becomes suspect turns out to be innocent of any wrongdoing. The wife and the audience are quite happy, then, because he is so charming and attractive, and the wife has never ceased being in love with him, even though at moments she is terrified.

What about *Kramer vs. Kramer?* The screenplay by Robert Benton won an Oscar as best screenplay adapted from another medium—in this case an adaptation from the novel by Avery Corman. It is a highly effective screenplay with the protagonist Kramer, enacted by Dustin Hoffman, pitted against his wife in a custody battle for his son whom she left with him when she walked out. The wife, played by Meryl Streep, does not physically return on screen as the antagonist until the court battle.

However, she is not overlooked. She watches the boy from a store across the street. This action on her part serves two purposes: Even though she has deserted the boy, she does care about him. Otherwise, the custody suit she initiates would not be credible. She must not forget him. Nor must the audience forget her. This is a part of skillful writing. She, the antagonist, cannot be out of the movie. She is a strong pivotal character who sets herself up as the opposition.

Time is needed for the development of the relationship between Kramer and his son. Conflict exists between them. The boy, missing his mother, is hostile to his father. A close tie must develop between father and son to make Kramer's court battle for the boy most meaningful. Yet the antagonist who will fight for the boy cannot be absent up to that point. This is an adroit handling of an antagonist who is not actively part of the story line for nearly half the picture and yet is the strong opposing force. (More on *Kramer vs. Kramer* will be discussed in "The Build," Chapter 7, and in "Resolution," Chapter 8.)

If you plan a story in which the brunt of the opposition needs to be deferred for essential development of another phase, without which the rest of the story cannot be told (e.g., that wonderful love relationship between father and son had to develop in order for Kramer to wage the custody battle for his son), you must plan the way for the antagonist to remain a part of the picture until the big counterthrust as the major striking force.

This type of story development is not the usual, but it can be effective with skillful writing. And during the antagonist's seemingly dormant phase, there is strong conflict—thrust and counterthrust between father and son—out of which the deep affection for one another, develops. That development is essential for Kramer to wage the court fight.

MUST THE ANTAGONIST BE HUMAN?

In all these antagonist examples, we are dealing with *people* as the opposition. It is the human menace who sets up the counterthrusts against the protagonist. But what about those antagonists who get no salary but add to production costs? What about the hurricane, the tidal wave, the raging fire, the earthquake? One often hears the question from students, Can the antagonist be environment?

Although environment can play a strong part in providing opposition to the protagonist, environment is inanimate. It cannot answer back. When an antagonist cannot answer back in human terms, genuine conflict between protagonist and antagonist cannot be sustained. For example, can an earthquake and only an earthquake as the opposition sustain interest? Let's look at the motion picture *Earthquake,* which has thrilled audiences from the time of its first run in movie houses to reruns on television. The earthquake would not have been enough in itself to sustain audience interest no matter how devastating it was (complete with thunderous Sensurround). The human conflicts— the people conflicts—are essential to hold interest as the earthquake's phases of destruction intensify.

The major personal conflict of the chief protagonist is with his wife. He is in love with another woman. Although the earthquake is the big overall antagonist, the triangle presents a subplot conflict. (Refer back to Chapter 3, "The Protagonist," on the subplots in disaster films.) These subplots—the play within a play—carry the interest in people conflicts. The audience needs to be absorbed in people and to be asking the question, What will happen to them? Will the girl trapped by the National Guardsman with intentions to rape her be rescued? Will our hero protagonist break from his wife and consolidate his love affair with his girlfriend?

The wife and the National Guardsman both are antagonists in these play-within-a-play subplots. These secondary plots serve as little independent dramas and sustain people interest. Over them all is the devastating force, the earthquake. It is a terrifying antagonist, but the inaminate force needs the human conflicts to nourish interest in itself.

Airport is another of the disaster-type motion pictures, with disaster threatening the lives of the passengers and crew aboard the big jet airliner. Subplots create protagonist-antagonist conflicts. These conflicts involving the people hold interest, while over it all is the bomb threat, complete with the unknown bomber aboard the plane. The identity of the bomber is a mystery that must be solved in order to find out where he has hidden the bomb and deactivate it in time. Thus a strong whodunit element is injected in the life-and-death suspense.

The mystery bomber with concealed bomb is the prime antagonist. But the personal, individual stories flesh out the pending disaster by presenting the human interest conflicts. One story involves the old lady, portrayed by Helen Hayes, who sneaks aboard the plane without a ticket. The antagonist is the airline employee who wants to abort her attempt to fly free. Her explanation—that she always sneaks on planes because she loves to travel but cannot afford the trips—wins audience sympathy and endows her with antihero stature, even though her story is one of the multiple subplots.

These individual stories are like branches of a tree; the tree's trunk is the major story line, of which the bomber and the bomb represent the antagonist force.

In *The Towering Inferno,* the raging fire in the skyscraper is the major antagonist. As the protagonist chief engineer battles desperately to prevent the fire from engulfing the tower where the party guests are gathered and trapped, the *Grand Hotel* technique of presenting many human dramas in one area is employed. Disaster films are particularly well suited to that technique because they are so big. But in any type of film, the nonpersonal antagonist, no matter how menacing, is not enough to sustain interest if human conflict is absent.

This important point is further illustrated in the motion picture *Jaws*. The killer shark is the antagonist, a terrible menacing force. Its strikes against swimmers holidaying at the seaside town leave grisly sights of chewed-off arms and legs on the bloody waters. When Police Chief Brody, the bounty hunter, and the oceanographer set out on the shark hunt, the terror of the shark mounts. There have been few such horrifying, thrill-packed spectacles as the deadly shark pitching against the boat, its massive jaws open (all $6,000,000 worth of mechanical shark that Universal built), its huge gnashing teeth ready to rip apart the vessel and its human riders.

Despite the tremendous excitement the shark provides audiences, the story line is far better sustained by the inclusion of strong human conflict: Police Chief Brody who wants the beaches closed versus the mayor who does not want to spoil the tourist trade. The bounty hunter is a conflict character, too. The oceanographer injects a lighter touch. The story line is ingenious. Although the mayor withdraws his opposition to closing the beaches, thus removing himself as a conflict force, the shark's killings intensify. Thus, the thrill-packed shark hunt reaches its highest degree of motivation, and the shark hunt pounds to the peak of suspense.

Herman Melville's classic *Moby Dick* concerns itself with the hunt for the Great White Whale. But the whale is not as active a destructive force as the shark in *Jaws*. This does not mean that the Great White Whale out there in the sea, ready to strike a ship at any encounter, is not a menace. But the destructive force is Captain Ahab and his obsessive drive to hunt down and kill the whale. His mad hunt for the Great White Whale twists his personality and stamps him as the antagonist. Protagonist Ishmael is a prime target of his cruelty, the result of the madness that twists Ahab. Mention *Moby Dick,* the novel or the motion picture adaptation (several remakes), and it brings to mind not the whale but Ahab. In the human element—Ahab's obsession—lies the strength of *Moby Dick*.

In the motion picture *Jeremiah Johnson,* screenplay by John Milius, the hero battles the frozen North. His attempts to survive would not sustain interest in an entire motion picture. Milius did not set out to tell that kind of story. A man trying to survive under such weather conditions would not have provided a star with a rich enough role, either. Nor is it likely that man against the weather, and only the weather, would have made a very interesting or exciting motion picture.

Jeremiah Johnson has Robert Redford in the role of the protagonist of that name, and the movie combines man's battle against the environment with engrossing human elements of conflict. Jeremiah Johnson establishes a love relationship with a woman. She and her little boy live with him in a hut. But when he returns to them after one of his excursions to hunt game for food and for other survival essentials, he finds the woman and the boy murdered.

Jeremiah sets out to track down their killer and take revenge. The human element of the murderer as antagonist, whom Jeremiah finds and with whom he engages in mortal combat, strengthens and sustains the screenplay. Once this phase of the story line is introduced, it propels the protagonist into a new, intense objective which takes precedence over the adverse environment and also gives richer dimension to the character of Jeremiah Johnson.

Remember: Any inanimate or nonhuman opposition—whether environment, killer beast, fish, or anything inanimate or nonpersonal—is not a sufficient antagonist for your motion picture or television script. The inanimate or otherwise impersonal menace should be reinforced by the human antagonist, so that both protagonist and antagonist can react and strengthen the conflicts. With little exception, the nonhuman antagonist as the sole counterforce offers a Johnny-one-note script, i.e., the one note of repetition, flawed in providing only nonpersonal opposition for the protagonist.

Neil Simon is a brilliant playwright and screenwriter. Most of his plays become motion pictures. His stage and screen hits began with *Come Blow Your Horn.* Simon has successfully adapted several of his stage plays into screenplays. He also wrote the original screenplay *The Out-of-Towners,* which missed.

The Out-of-Towners lacks a single strong objective for the protagonist. He wants his business stay in New York to run a smooth course. This in itself is too general an objective. There is no real single purpose—something personal that he wants urgently to attain.

The choice of antagonist misses fire, too. This antagonist is the city. His stay in the city is hampered by inconveniences such as mix-ups in hotel reservations, and he is further besieged by being mugged in Central Park.

Because *The Out-of-Towners* otherwise lacks a central story line in which the protagonist attempts to drive toward his goal and the antagonist hurtles counterthrusts blocking progressive moves, the protagonist's chief action is an inactive screaming and shouting that he is going to sue. It was an unfortunate choice of roles for that fine actor Jack Lemmon, since his protagonist role offered little more than those outbursts of angry frustration. Nor can the city answer with actions that could give the protagonist challenging action that would move the story ahead. This further points out how the environment itself, minus the human conflict, becomes ineffective.

THE ANTAGONIST WITHIN

Another question asked by writing students about the *human* conflict is whether a person—the whole individual—must present the antagonist opposition. This is not always the case. Sometimes the human element can be a character trait. Sometimes a trait can create a strong conflict or war within oneself. A striking example is *Rocky,* the original screenplay written by and starring Sylvester Stallone. *Rocky* was judged the best original screenplay at the Academy Awards in 1978.

Rocky's major struggle is with the loser aspect of himself. His environment is a poor one, and he hustles his living making collections for a loan shark. His primary interest is in prizefighting, but his boxing career has lifted him no more than a short distance from the mat. In an early scene, his fight trainer walks out on him, telling him that he will never get anywhere as a fighter. Rocky bolsters his own morale by telling anyone who will listen (hardly anyone!) that he has just won a fight. This is a fight that takes place in a shoddy gym with a small-time opponent of Rocky's status and leads to the trainer's writing Rocky off.

To add to his frustrations and humiliations is a brother who is critical of him. This is the entire patchwork of Rocky's life, a patchwork bearing the label *loser*.

But suddenly, life takes a golden turn. A boxing champion needs promotion for his next fight, and a publicity stunt is arranged for him. He will fight an unknown, a typical Joe Q. Public citizen. Rocky is picked as his opponent, and this is the stuff of which dreams are made. He has a chance to fight the champ. But the champion who gives him this opportunity is not the antagonist. Remember: Rocky's big enemy is his bad environment, his downbeat life, the loser in himself.

Even though the champion will be Rocky's opponent in the ring, the champ has set in motion a positive side of Rocky's life by giving him the opportunity to fight. Rocky has purpose now and a hope. His morale receives a tremendous boost. He goes into training for the big fight. The trainer who walked out on him returns to help him get in shape, and as Rocky trains, toning his muscles and developing boxing skill, his confidence builds. Romance also enters his life. The attractive young woman with whom he falls in love and who shares his love gives incentive to his life.

On Rocky's last day of training, he looks and feels like a champion. Audiences feel it, too. They share his hope and his confidence and see the steady development of his fighting strength. But can he win? The night before the fight, he faces the reality of it in the form of self-doubt. The self-doubt is the loser within him; it has always been in him as the antagonist in his life.

The self-doubt also has a basis in the reality of the entire prospect of fighting the champion. Rocky's self-doubt, coupled with the reality of the fight he faces, prompts him to tell his girl that he knows he cannot win the fight. The most he can hope for is to last fifteen rounds. This serves as the antagonist counterthrust that leaves the protagonist in the questionable and very suspenseful situation of whether he will stay the fifteen rounds.

Take notice, too, that the counterthrust (Rocky's self-doubt) comes after the very positive forward thrust of Rocky's full confidence. Both of these moves are obligatory in building interest and suspense, the "What's going to happen next and will the protagonist gain his objective?" that is so essential in every script. (Chapter 7, "The Build," further discusses this essential aspect of the script.) Also note that the antagonist in Rocky does not stand alone, but is intertwined with people involved with Rocky.

In the motion picture *"10,"* written, produced, and directed by Blake Edwards (of "Pink Panther" fame), the protagonist, (played by Dudley Moore) is also plagued by a character trait antagonist. As he reaches his fortieth birthday, he develops a fear of losing his sexual drive. He has the desperate desire to prove himself sexually.

This propels him into the high comedy of pursuing a beautiful young woman whom he glimpses in a car on her way to her own wedding. Driving past her in his car, he becomes instantly enamored of her. His over-forty complex also places him in additional conflicts. He acts out his fears by breaking up with his girlfriend, Samantha, portrayed by Julie Andrews. Since she is close to his own age, he no longer finds her desirable. However, she is not opposing him. She does not offer obstacles in his pursuit of his sexual objective.

Nor is the girl he fancies he wants and about whom he also fantasizes a tangible obstacle in his path. When finally, after pursuing her to Mexico on her honeymoon, he does get together with her, she imposes harsh requirements for his performing the sex act that he cannot meet. He cannot keep up with the musical accompaniment of Ravel's *Bolero.*

His acceptance of his middle age takes him back full circle to Samantha. Both women support the story line, building the interest and enabling the conflicts to be expressed in human terms. The antagonist—which is the protagonist's fear of losing his sexual drive—needs these tangible people conflicts against which to play off. Just as the inanimate or nonhuman antagonist cannot stand alone to be effective, character traits also need to be played off against tangible people conflicts.

An example of a smaller motion picture which is sensitive but lacking the elements of tangible people conflict is *The Old Man and the Sea,* adapted into a screenplay from Ernest Hemingway's short novel. Fearing old age and diminishing physical strength, the old fisherman sets out in his boat to capture one specific, huge fish. This pitches him and his small boat into a dangerous, arduous task. However, the lack of crosscurrents of conflicts with other people as tangible antagonistic elements narrows the degree of interest.

The portrayal of the old man battling the sea and the huge fish, set against his old age and waning strengh, contains the compelling force of Hemingway's literary magic. But it remains a small, though sensitive, motion picture that in today's market might not have found a production.

A CHECKLIST FOR YOUR WRITING

Make sure that the counterthrusts of the antagonist are tangible and strong enough opposition against the forward action of the protagonist, who is attempting to achieve his objective. The protagonist versus antagonist pattern producing cross-conflicts is essential to your story line as shown below:

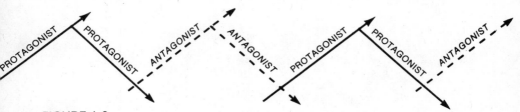

FIGURE 4-3.

Be certain that your screenplay or teleplay incorporates this basic pattern. Without the cross-conflicts sustained progressively throughout your work, the script will be flat and uninteresting.

Imagine two people together, talking. What you have is conversation. But let them clash. Give them conflict, and you inject interest, excitement, and suspense.

The following are some helpful ways in which you can check your work. Ask yourself:

Who is my protagonist? What is the urgent need of my protagonist—the goal that he must attain?

Is this urgent need—the something the protagonist desperately wants—sufficiently motivated? Is the motivation believable?

Does the motivation fit the characterization (character traits) of the protagonist?

Do I create an empathetic bond between protagonist and the viewer? Will the audience care about my protagonist and root for my protagonist to win?

What about my antagonist? Can I clearly identify the antagonist? (Ask yourself this question, because you must be clear and definite about the antagonist in order to give this antagonist the clear-cut counterthrusts so essential to the conflict that must keep building to sustain interest in the work.)

Once you have the protagonist and antagonist clearly defined in terms of who they are and their aims—protagonist objective versus counterthrust—you will ask where you should start your script.

Where *do* you start?

5

The Start—
Where the Problem Begins

It is not uncommon for new writers to begin their first script without setting up conflict or giving even an indication of what the story is about. When the writing student is asked what the story is about, generally the answer is that the story is all there, the entire plot in hand, and it will all begin to unfold in twenty pages. In the case of a teleplay, the student will give the assurance that it's all there starting with the second act.

Waiting until the second act of a television script—no matter what length—or equivalent timing in a screenplay, will turn off the home viewer and in the theater produce other negative reactions. Therefore, it is essential right from the start that the work does catch and hold interest. But first, before a teleplay or screenplay reaches production, it must grab and retain the interest of the person or persons responsible for buying the script. As a rule of thumb, the script editor or producer can tell within three to five pages of reading whether the work merits continued reading.

THE TEASER

The work must catch instant interest. Therefore, the action of your story must start right at the point where your story begins. It needs an instant hook—the grabber, in television known as the "tease" or "teaser." The opening scene must tease the viewer. In most teleplay shows ranging from the hour to the longer forms, the first commercial is introduced right after the teaser. That means that the teaser must be so provocative that the viewer is interested enough to sit through the commercial in order to see what happens next in this enticing teleplay. But whether or not the opening scene represents the teaser leading to the commercial, or into the rest of the first act, it must catch and hold interest.

The motion picture industry does not employ the working term *teaser*. But the first scene before the credits roll and following up while the credits are still rolling needs to be a grabber. Keep this in mind always: The provocative opening scene, by whatever name it is called, is the start of your script—the point of action where the story you want to tell must begin. Your teleplay or motion picture must not begin a moment earlier or later than that point. Television and motion picture writing are disciplined forms. Audience interest is sustained only by what happens on the screen from the moment it happens in the story you expect to tell.

Let's look at some of these provocative opening scenes. In the motion picture *Dog Day Afternoon* (screenplay by Frank Pierson), Sonny (Al Pacino) drives up to a bank with two companions, Sal and Jackie. They are a compelling trio, intent on a purpose, even as they engage in matters pertaining to their appearance: hair combing, tie adjusting, flicking cuffs. Sonny also makes sure that the curl that drops on his forehead is in place. Obviously, they want to look their best for a grand entrance. In another moment they stage their big entrance into the bank. Sonny saunters over to a customer table and fills out a deposit slip, Jackie beside him, his eyes darting over the scene. Immediately, the audience is intrigued by what is happening here. Sonny's casualness contrasts with Jackie's wariness. And where is Sal? Suddenly, attention rivets on him. Whipping out a gun, he points it at the bank manager. The robbery of the bank has begun.

This is the provocative beginning for *Dog Day Afternoon*. The start of the robbery is the springboard of this comedy-drama in which everything does not turn out as envisioned by Sonny, the leader. By taking hostages and locking them in the vault, he expects to make a swift, safe getaway. But, he is repeatedly thwarted, even as he seems to make progress in negotiations with police, namely Detective Moretti. The script builds suspensefully and not without humor, for Sonny is quite a fellow. The motion picture has begun right at the point of action—when the robbery begins. The story involves what happens from that point on.

In "Downhill to Death," an episode of the television show "Hart to Hart" written by Bill and Jo LaMond, Jennifer Hart is in a restaurant in which she combines lunch and her interview with a rock star. She overhears a woman and man in the next booth planning the murder of the man's wife. The crime is to be committed on the ski trails of Vail. Preventing the murder becomes the objective of the Harts, who head for Vail and the ski trails. The teleplay does not begin a moment earlier, or it would be too soon for the story it tells.

A good proportion of television crime shows and detective–police investigator motion pictures have a crime being committed as the opening scene. The second scene of this type of show usually sets in motion the investigator, perhaps a private detective or a police homicide investigator in shows starring such a character as protagonist.

An exception is the show "Columbo," starring Peter Falk, which is still seen late nights on television, although its popular long run has ended. A murder is committed in the opening scene, but the format of "Columbo" has always required that the murderer make elaborate preparations to cover his tracks. Such an elaborate and cunning cover-up thus requires Columbo to use to the fullest his brilliant police investigation talents. It also differs in pattern from other police shows in that the detailed action of the murderer in covering his tracks generally takes a solid fifteen minutes of playing time before Columbo is on the case. But the point of action leads right into the murder, and this is where each episode has begun.

"The Watch Commander," an episode of "Police Story," opens with the provocative scene of Don Carpenter, a police officer, awakening in the middle of the night and rousing his wife. He has heard strange sounds. He will check the house and grounds while she looks in on their children. He cautions her to stay indoors and away from the window. But hearing three shots after he steps outside, she hurries out. He tells her that he fired the shots at three youthful prowlers. However, they got away.

Although he does not notice her reaction, her expression is one of desperation. It is obvious to the viewer that something is wrong with this police officer, and that his wife is aware of the problem. In the next scene, she calls on a police sergeant friend of Carpenter's to tell him that it has happened again. This is the core of the story, and Mark Rodgers, who won an award for the script, starts his story not at the earlier time when Don Carpenter had fired at unseen prowlers, but at the point of action of the story which he tells in dramatic script terms.

In the opening scene of "The Gift," an episode written by Carol Evan McKeand (from a story by Ray Goldrup and Jack Hanrahan) and shown on "The Waltons" television series, the teenage Seth and his mother are visiting the Walton family and are listening to the radio with them, eagerly awaiting the country and western music program featuring Seth's father, a singer. Seth, planning to join his father, wants to be a musician like him. As a first step in his musical career, he is anxious to make a record. He and John Boy (who, played by Richard Thomas, was still a regular on the show) decide to start out early the next morning to cut some wood. As the boys set their plan, Seth's mother reminds him that he had been ill and cautions him not to overstrain.

This starts the script, the provocative opening scene catching immediate viewer interest in Seth and also paving the way for the highly dramatic human problem. During the cutting of the wood, Seth collapses. That he is terminally ill, as diagnosed by the doctor, intensifies the problem that is the main story line of the script. His reaction to the knowledge of his impending death and the reaction of the Walton family build the script. The episode did not begin with the arrival of Seth and his mother at the Waltons or with their tuning in the radio program. Either beginning would not be close enough to the point of action. The opening scene leads right into Seth's collapse and also tells what is pertinent to the action of the script. This advances the plot line. The drama is in motion at the point where the action begins.

Episodes of "The Waltons" do not set up a formal teaser opening scene, followed by the commercial. The teleplays open directly on Act 1. Each week a voice-over introduces the episode, briefly setting the mood and background of the show and provocatively offering the theme of that episode. The voice belongs to Earl Hamner, Jr., who wrote *The Homecoming,* a book about his growing up in West Virginia in the 1930s during the Great Depression. The book became a television feature film and then the weekly series. The weekly voice-over is not a teaser. In a sense, though, it teases by suggesting the theme and action.

The voice-over of *Brian's Song* (a television feature film by William Blinn first shown in motion picture theaters) is a brief narration at the start of the film that tells the viewer that this is the story of friendship and also a story of life and death. It is a compelling introduction, serving a double purpose. As the voice-over is heard, the story begins at the action point. The camera follows a taxi as it travels on a winding road to its destination, a football practice field. The viewer knows that this is a practice field because the camera picks up the players in action on the field. As Gale Sayers, a major character in *Brian's Song,* steps out of the taxi, a football is kicked out of bounds and narrowly misses hitting him. He tosses the ball back to Brian Piccolo, whose story this is and who then introduces himself to Sayers. The scene begins the story in conflict between them and also with the suggestion that friendship will result, which is the theme of the show. Their meeting takes less than two minutes of playing time.

From the football field of *Brian's Song,* let us move to the main street of a frontier town and an episode of "Gunsmoke," a Western series staring James Arness that enjoyed a seventeen-year first run on television. In the early 1970s it was the last of the popular Western shows to be canceled. At that time all opening scenes of scripts for the show were called "teasers," and each was followed by the commercial. However, the teaser format for the show was soon eliminated because a "nonviolent" programming phase was initiated in the industry. This was the first of several nonviolent phases which eventually led to the establishment of the strongly contested "family hour."

In the opening scene of the "Gunsmoke" script "Lucius Prince of Philadelphia," by Jack Miller, a door bursts open and an elderly man is booted out onto the main street. At first glance he would be considered another drunken bum. But the careful way in which he brushes himself off after he gets back on his feet shows that he is accustomed to a better style of living. His attire, too, bears a suggestion of good quality. But whoever he is, in another moment he is shot at. Fortunately for him, the shot misses, and it gives him time to start running for his life.

Meantime, the television viewer is let in on who is shooting at him. Tom Rickaby, the assailant, is joined by an attractive woman who has heard the shot but does not know that Rickaby, her fiancé, has tried to kill the old man. He does tell her that he has seen Prince. It is obvious that they have been looking for the old man; Rickaby now thinks he would take flight to the next town, Dodge City. Rickaby and the girl are not aware that a stagecoach has left the main street with Lucius Prince aboard; a canvas hides him from their view. This is the last camera shot the viewer sees as the teaser ends. Taking scarcely over three minutes of playing time, the story has begun at the esssential point of action, not a moment before or after. What happens to Lucius Prince from then on constitutes the major thread of the story.

Situation comedies must also start at a provocative point of action to hold viewer interest. A "Taxi" script has Louie, the dispatcher, tell the drivers gathered in the garage (as usual) that Alex has been shot. As evidence, Alex comes in with a bandage on his left ear: A passenger has shot him. Thus, within the mere moments it has taken to establish this situation, Alex's problem is established. Alex is the protagonist in this episode, and because of the shooting he develops a fear of driving a cab in New York. This is his problem, intensifying to the point of his quitting his job to become a waiter.

The script opens directly at the point of action, shortly after the shooting. If the script had opened on the shooting in Alex's cab, it would have been irrelevant to the main story line. It is Alex's reaction to the shooting and what happens to him after it, not the incident itself, that starts the story.

Another "Taxi" script places Louie as the protagonist with the urgent need to send his mother to Las Vegas to absorb the sunshine of the warm climate for her health. The runty dispatcher's objective is established at the start of the script in a phone conversation with his mother. Enter the antagonist, Louie's gambler brother on his way to Las Vegas. He refuses to take their mother to the gambler's paradise, so Louie attempts to force him to make that commitment by pitting Alex and his card-playing expertise against the brother. If he loses, the brother has to abide by the commitment to the mother. With the main story line, Louie's plan for his mother and the conflict involving his brother, you can see that the half-hour script needs to start at the action point, where Louie promises to send his mother to Las Vegas and the brother thwarts the promise.

In an episode of the top-rated "All in the Family" (now "Archie Bunker's Place"), Edith (played by Jean Stapleton) loses her locket. Although the jewelry, a gift from her grandmother, has strong sentimental value for her, she assures Archie that it is worth only about ten dollars. Archie places a higher value of two hundred dollars on it. His purpose is to collect from the company with which he has insured the necklace. Out of this the complications develop. For this story line development, the script opens at the start of the action. This action point is the loss of the necklace and Archie's intentions of collecting on the higher value he places on it. This pertinent situation is set up in the first moments of the script.

An outstanding episode in the same series is the attempted rape of Edith. The opening moments allow for Archie and Mike to leave the house to check on Archie's new place of business— the bar. It is essential for Edith to be alone in the house for her confrontation with the rapist. Therefore, the segment begins close to the point where the major story line starts to develop. That the segment has been expanded into an hour from the half-hour format does not allow more time to reach the starting point of action. The extra time allows more development of complications out of the attempted rape. The starting point of the episode must still lead right into the action.

THE DAWDLER

Be aware, however, that in contrast to this excellent expanded episode, some of the long forms—feature films made for television—dawdle their way to the point where the story really begins. A television feature dealing with the life of Amelia Earhart provides such an example. At least twenty minutes (nearly the entire first act) takes her through childhood into adulthood. This is the life of a world-famous flier. Her life was dedicated to aviation. But her youthful years in the script indicate barely any interest in flying.

She is depicted as a child sliding down boxes on a table toboggan. Obviously, this is to show that she had an early interest in motion and in flying objects. However, not until the end of the first act does she evince any interest in an actual plane. She is an adult (probably twenty or twenty-one) when this "great event" takes place. Walking down the street with a girl friend, she looks up to the sky. Something catches her interest. Excited, she tells her friend to look up. She also points to the object in the sky: It's a plane in flight. Most likely, this observation was written into the script to show the whipping up of Amelia's interest in flying. Unfortunately, even by the end of the first act, the television feature is not even on the runway.

Another television feature film provided, as a capsule preview of the story, the struggle of a woman to gain control of the business her husband headed before he suffered a heart attack and subsequently died. Interesting? Provocative? So it seemed. A viewer would expect the quick demise of the husband and the strong drama of conflict dealing with the power struggle the wife faces. But the husband does not even have his heart attack until well into the first act. Then, for an interminably long time in terms of lagging interest in the show, the husband lies dying on his hospital bed. It takes a long time for him to die.

Not until the last half hour of the feature does the wife's fight for control of the business begin. The battle for control and her victory do liven up the script considerably, but the conflict is thin and arrives much too late. No matter what length the script, it must start at the point of action to win interest.

WHAT MAKES AN OPENING GRABBER?

Of the interesting made-for-television movies, *That Certain Summer,* starring Hal Holbrook as the protagonist, is one that launches the action from a springboard in the opening scene. The protagonist is a homosexual. His son, who does not know this, plans to visit him. A strong father-son conflict develops because the father's lover unexpectedly moves in with him. The provocative beginning leads right into the major conflict of this excellent film.

The average motion picture is two hours in length. But just as in the teleplay, which should capture interest from the start no matter what length, the screenplay also needs to begin its story at the provocative point of action.

In *One Flew Over the Cuckoo's Nest,* the camera picks up some of the inmates at a mental institution and quickly cuts to the outside of the building and the door through which the protagonist McMurphy (Jack Nicholson) is escorted under guard. He has been arrested and convicted of a crime, but before he will serve his sentence in prison or in the mental institution, it must be determined whether or not he is sane. He will spend time under observation in the psychiatric hospital so the authorities can decide what to do with him. McMurphy is a brash fellow, and so the contrast between his personality and outlook and that of the other downbeat, sad sack inmates is quickly established. So is the hook, for the introduction of the cocky McMurphy, the study to be made on him, and the doleful inmates capture immediate interest in the film.

The moment McMurphy sets eyes on his new companions, he

is determined to liberate their minds and their bodies. Against him is Nurse Ratched and it becomes McMurphy and the liberation he expects to effect versus the archantagonist and the institution she represents as the head nurse. The film has begun well at the point of action that leads directly into Hauben and Goldman's absorbing and powerful screenplay. If the script had begun earlier, such as at the point when the court decision was made concerning McMurphy, it would have started the story too early. The moment when McMurphy is entering the institution is the right time.

Notice that no explanation of why McMurphy was arrested is given at the opening action. The explanation is not important at this point—the point of action where the major plot line begins.

But since it is well for McMurphy's complex character to be more fully rounded out, the crimes for which McMurphy had drawn that first sentence to a work farm are not omitted from the screenplay. A section further on in this chapter discusses this aspect.

On the other hand, the arrest of Billy, the young American, at an airport in Turkey is an early scene in the Oscar-winning motion picture *Midnight Express*. He is caught smuggling heroin. The opening scene shows him strapping the drug packages to his body, and in a tense scene at the airport he is apprehended. Such a beginning is the action point. That is where the major plot line begins—the story of Billy's harrowing prison experience and his desperate attempts to gain his freedom. McMurphy has a different objective—to liberate his fellow inmates in as much a psychological as a physical sense. *One Flew Over the Cuckoo's Nest* begins with the quick setting of his goal.

A strange sight awaits a group of military men in the space program as they arrive at a spaceship's landing site. Dead bodies of space travelers strewn over the area make up the provocative opening of *The Andromeda Strain*. This motion picture, adapted from Michael Crichton's novel, describes the scientific attempts to determine what type of virus or germ has fatally infected the spacemen.

Finding the men dead from something that happened to them

in outer space sets the story line at the point of action, for the crack research team assembled to combat the menace must learn what the invading organism is, why two people survived, and how to destroy the menace. However, despite the provocative begining, the film does not live up to its expectations. Instead, it bogs down into a type of medical treatise with the impersonal mystery virus as the primary antagonist. A human antagonist—a woman scientist—emerges later, but the conflict is not strong enough or well enough defined.

When *Star Wars* opened at first-run theaters throughout the nation, box office receipts everywhere reached an all-time high in movie history. The opening scene is a space battle which results in the kidnapping of the princess. *Star Wars* opens exactly at the point of action of the rousing space adventure.

So does another motion picture, also of very big hit proportions: *Jaws*. A woman steps out of her beachfront cottage for a late-night swim. It is a fatal one. She is attacked and killed by a shark. This horrifying tease scene opens *Jaws* at the action point of the story. The menace of the shark is the basis of *Jaws*. As discussed in an earlier chapter, it provokes the police chief into wanting to close the beaches and puts him in conflict with the mayor as the story builds in cumulative excitement.

The opening scene of the motion picture *Deliverance* follows a group of men driving to the river. A canoe is strapped on top of each car. This beginning, the men's embarkation on what is meant to be a happy holiday trip, sets up the adventure of melodramatic dimensions. What happens to them on this river trip—the holiday that turns into grim drama—is the story.

The motion picture *Heaven Can Wait*, with screenplay by Warren Beatty and Elaine May (a remake of *Here Comes Mr. Jordan*), introduces the protagonist as a star football player (Beatty) who, when riding home from the playing field on his bike, meets with an accident in a tunnel collision. He is dead, but not quite dead. All he needs to stay alive is someone else's living body. (His own has already been cremated.) His stepping into the body of an intended murder victim who has not quite expired builds the complications of this entertaining film that begins at the action point. Our hero-protagonist has to be killed off early in the film because the story line concerns what happens to him in his new identity.

"*10*," the motion picture comedy by Blake Edwards (writer-director-producer), opens on the protagonist (Dudley Moore) entering his pitch-dark apartment and, after lighting a match, groping his way into the living room. This is a tease, an immediate attention grabber. Anything can happen to him in this blackout. Will he be hit on the head? Will he be shot?

Since this is a comedy, the lights flash on. It is a surprise party. A crowd of friends joyously shout a happy birthday greeting at him. But to him the event is catastrophe. Blowing out the large number of candles on his birthday cake, he is hit by the realization that he is forty years old. It is a shocking age—much too old. It is an age when he feels he must prove to himself that he has not lost his sexual drive and his manhood. This opening scene sets the course of action of "*10*," starting the film at the action point.

From this point, he embarks on his desperate objective of proving his manhood with the girl to whom he gives the perfect rating ten. This lively comedic motion picture opens right into the story it sets out to tell.

Walking brightly into her Manhattan apartment with a bag of groceries, Pamela of *The Goodbye Girl* receives a shock. A brief note from her live-in lover tells her that he has left her. As if this were not bad enough news, she is confronted by the new man to whom Tony, her former lover, has signed over the lease of the apartment. After first trying to evict her, the new lessee allows her and her young daughter to share the apartment with him under certain conditions. Because the film story is about this young woman to whom men say goodbye and what happens to her with her new roommate, the story gets under way immediately with her meeting him under these trying circumstances.

Think of this: What if the movie had opened on a scene in which Tony is personally breaking the news to Pamela that he is leaving her? Or a scene of Tony leasing the apartment to the new male tenant? With either scene, the film would not have begun at the action point. Neil Simon is too skillful to have begun his film at any other point except where the story begins. Blake Edwards did not open *"10"* until his protagonist turned forty and set his desperate goal. Scripts that do not capture immediate interest also usually fail to develop in an interesting fashion. How can they when they don't step directly into the action of the story?

THE EFFECTIVE (AND NOT SO EFFECTIVE) FLASHBACK

What about flashbacks? This is a question that writing students are likely to ask. If you are writing the type of script that can only be dramatized effectively through the backward look, be certain that you open with a scene that captures immediate interest. Remember: That scene must be so provocative that it will hold attention through a flashback.

Avoid the flashback that will throw your protagonist into a state of reminiscing of things past. Do not have your protagonist looking out the window at the snowfall and remembering another snowfall in which . . . (and the story unfolds). This is a misuse of the flashback, serving only as a crutch to tell the story. It does not catch interest, nor is there any reason to believe such a flashback beginning can sustain interest, since it does not open at a point of action. The flashback technique does not change the fact that the script must open at the provocative point of action. The opening scene that leads to the flashback must be a tease into it. The flashback lead-in should be at some critical point in the protagonist's life. A decision must be made or a verdict awaited. The outcome of life-and-death surgery may hang in the balance. This is the critical stuff of flashback.

The motion picture *Serpico* opens in gripping fashion: Serpico has been shot. An ambulance speeds him to the hospital's emergency room. This provocative beginning intrigues audiences. What happened? Why has he been shot? It is also quickly revealed in the opening seconds of the film that he is a policeman. But the emphasis on his name indicates that this is no average police officer. Serpico is known; that name means something. It stirs extraordinary excitement among the people who hear the news. Indeed, Serpico is a name to arouse interest. And why—why has he been shot?

At this critical point, the highly dramatic story is told in flashback. Joining the New York police force, Serpico finds himself in a fight against corruption. He cannot accept the payoffs that his fellow officers take as part of the work. In opposing corruption, he bucks tremendous odds. The forces against him become too powerful, and finally, in desperation, he goes public and tells his story to a newspaper. The shooting is the attempt to silence him permanently and also to set an example for others who may refuse to fall in line with the corruption. But notice that the actual act of shooting him does not open the film. This is not the point of action. The major story line is not concerned with tracking down the gunman who shot him, but with how it happened and why.

The same techniques of good scriptwriting must also be applied to the flashback. When you have the provocative opening scene and then flash back to tell your story, that story must also begin at a point of action. After the provocative lead-in scene in any story, the writer also must start the major story at the provocative point.

Another excellent example of the use of flashback is in *Babe,* the television feature based on the life of a famous female athlete. The provocative opening scene has Babe undergoing critical surgery for cancer. Will she live or die? This scene leaves the element of suspense as the story flashes back into the life of Babe and her climb to success. The script carries her career suspensefully to the dramatic opening that led into the flashback—the surgery.

Babe survives the operation and determines to resume her athletic career. Thus, the film enters another suspenseful phase of her life. The story thrusts forward, the viewer absorbed in whether or not Babe can make her comeback. This is skillful scriptwriting. Note how the flashback thrusts the story forward to the point-of-action opening that led into it. With Babe's recovery from the crucial surgery, the feature film carries itself forward with the interest held in whether or not Babe will again succeed. The antagonist is the illness. Babe is battling for a comeback against that health threat. In that respect the film has strong conflict and suspense.

Babe and *Serpico* effectively employ the flashback, and so do a number of other teleplays and motion pictures. But keep in mind that the flashback should be used sparingly. Few story lines lend themselves to the flashback technique. The flashback is not a crutch that the writer can lean on to explain how the major characters reach the critical point from where the story would flash back.

Only in special storytelling situations is the flashback technique employed. Be careful. Don't rush into a flashback as the way to unfold your teleplay or screenplay story. Even if you should use the flashback, don't lose sight of the fact that the script must move forward—in thrusts and counterthrusts providing conflict scene by scene—and that a script must start at the point where the story begins—the point of action.

But, you ask, How do I explain to the viewer what went on before my script opens at the point of action? This is the moment when your story begins. This is the time when the protagonist wants something urgently, only to be confronted by a problem in obtaining his objective because the antagonist blocks him. But what brought protagonist and antagonist to this point of action that opens the script? What went before?

The following chapter deals with this phase of your writing: what went before.

6

Exposition

Webster's dictionary offers this definition of *exposition:* "the act or practice of exposing." In scripting your teleplay or screenplay, exposition is the exposing or revealing to the home viewer or theater audience the necessary information concerning what went on before your story began.

Except in the weekly television series shows, characters introduced on the screen have never been seen before. Who are they? How did they get in the situation confronting them when the show begins? This is the sleight of hand; the audience does not see and is not aware of how it's being done. But there is no magic about it. It's part of skillful writing, well-crafted work. The handling of exposition in the script can be likened to the weaving or lacing in of threads of a pattern without showing the stitches. You do not put your story "on hold" while you give your characters the explanatory dialogue.

EXAMPLES OF EXPOSITION

In the previous chapter we discussed the point-of-action, provocative opening of Neil Simon's *The Goodbye Girl.* Audiences are introduced to Pamela on screen as she hurries down a street, carrying a big bag of groceries. The street is recognizable to most filmgoers. It looks like a street of The City—New York. That Pamela fits in as a resident is obvious from the bag of groceries she carries and because she enters an apartment building. She lives there. That is all audiences know about this attractive resident of Manhattan.

But on Pamela's entering her apartment, a child calls to her and waves a note. She is Pamela's daughter, as the filmgoers now know. The little girl also shrieks at her mother that it's happened again.

Tony has left, and he left a note for her. In this farewell note, Tony bids her good-bye, telling her he has gone to Hollywood. This is exposition, establishing Pamela as the "Goodbye Girl" who men leave, and also setting her in the performing arts. Her ex-lover is an actor. That it happened before is also further defined.

Her marriage broke up with her husband walking out. Now, as described in the previous chapter, the opening scene is the point of action. The next moment, a new man enters her life as antagonist. Conflict is developing with his announcement to her that the apartment is his and that he wants her to move out.

The confrontation with him is not exposition: It advances the story. But the confrontation draws out more information about them. They decide on a compromise. Pamela, with her little girl, will share the apartment with him. But she has conditions. She sets down house rules with which she expects him to conform. This is another bit of exposition, through which the audience learns about her lifestyle. More exposition follows, because instead of accepting her directives, he sets down *his* house rules that he expects *her* to follow. His house rules reveal his lifestyle, such as playing the guitar nude at three in the morning. She should keep her little girl from walking in on him. Exposition weaves important character traits of the major characters into an amusing conflict scene as the story moves ahead.

You will find opportunities in writing your script to weave in the exposition so that the stitches won't show. As you unfold your story, reveal the information at the time it needs to be known. The spots you select for the expository weaving will fit naturally, because your story will be under way.

Sight and Sound Exposition

A beautiful piece of exposition using sight and only musical sound is illustrated in the motion picture *Five Easy Pieces*, an original screenplay by Carol Eastman and starring Jack Nicholson. The introduction to the protagonist is as a hard hat worker on an oil derrick with a girlfriend and a pal who works alongside him. This is all that is known about him until he receives a letter that his father has taken ill. He decides that he must take the trip home. The trip to see his father is not expository.

That he travels home advances the story. The film gives a further glimpse into his life, but this is only a speck of information. It becomes obvious that he left home and his hometown to follow his own lifestyle. But what kind of life had he left?

As he drives, his car is stalled in a bumper-to-bumper traffic jam. Ahead of him, also stalled in traffic, is an open delivery truck with a piano on it. Now remember, he has been identified in the film thus far as a hard hat worker. His companions match this milieu. Suddenly, this hard hat worker dashes out of his car, climbs on the back of the truck, sits down at the piano, and plays with a true musician's skill. What's more, this is classical music of the concert pianist. Here is exposition illustrating that a picture speaks more than a thousand words. Through one brief scene at the piano (without dialogue), the audience is treated to excellent music at the same time that important information (exposition) is delivered about the protagonist.

That he has abandoned his musical career to pursue his own freewheeling lifestyle needs to be known at this point because it is a major conflict in the story into which he is heading. Sight and sound exposition is blended nicely into the story line.

Think of the static scene of dialogue that exposition might otherwise have required for the protagonist to explain to his pal or his girlfriend about his past life back home. But the screenwriter displayed enough originality and skill to avoid what could otherwise have been heavy-handed.

Use of Dialogue

Not every script lends itself to an opportune time for sight and sound exposition. When exposition needs to be accomplished with dialogue—as it usually does—strong conflict that keeps advancing the story gives the explanation a neat fit. In a "Columbo" television segment, a musician is not in conflict with his lifestyle in terms of his musical career. Rather than break up with his wife (as his girlfriend demands) and lose the money in her family, he kills the girl to silence her. Only when he is ready to kill does his triangular involvement become known. His girl-friend's argument with him is expository. The dialogue is conflict, woven directly into the story and advancing the action into murder.

The motion picture *And Justice for All* introduces a fighting lawyer protagonist (Al Pacino) in jail. Conditions are deplor-able, but audiences are given only moments to wonder why this clean-cut, intelligent-looking young man has been locked up. What crime has he committed? The explanation is given in brief, sharp dialogue in the quick time that he is released in the opening scene. He is a lawyer who punched Judge Fleming in the jaw during a courtroom case, and Fleming, a tough man to oppose under any circumstances, ordered him to jail. In his release, the young lawyer is cautioned not to tangle with the judge again. This is exposition that sets up the judge as antagonist and prepares the audience for the courtroom scene shortly after, with the continuing fury of Judge Fleming against this lawyer who is crusading for justice.

How Much Exposition?

The cause of McMurphy's arrest in *One Flew Over the Cuckoo's Nest* is not explained at the point of action opening. What does need to be known is that he is being placed in the mental institution to test his sanity. He becomes involved in liberating the inmates, as was discussed in "The Start," Chapter 5. But, as suggested in that discussion, the offenses for which he was arrested and convicted are later revealed. The major story line has been established. The audience is won over quickly to this brash, likable fellow and roots for him to achieve his objective. Then, in the later scene where one Dr. John M. Spivey of the State Hospital is evaluating McMurphy's case, with McMurphy in his office, the doctor reviews the criminal acts that had caused McMurphy to be convicted and sentenced to the work farm—he was charged with five assaults and with a statuatory rape that has McMurphy protesting that the girl told him she was eighteen—all after-the-fact. Judgment has been passed.

This is in the nature of exposition woven into the story line that had begun provocatively. More of a directive is also given McMurphy as to how his fate would be determined—the determination of whether he was really insane or faking the psychosis. The ultimatum moves the story line again from the brief moments of exposition into the drama that needs to build—and does, to powerful effect.

In contrast, the motion picture *Escape from Alcatraz* does not at all tell us for what crime the protagonist (played by Clint Eastwood) is sentenced to imprisonment on the Rock. His urgent objective is to escape from the island prison, and the audience is in full sympathy with him to achieve his goal.

Differently from the above two pictures, *The Last Detail,* a motion picture also starring Jack Nicholson as protagonist, does weave exposition concerning a crime and a sentence into its opening scene. This exposition is basic to the story. The navy protagonist and one of his buddies in his outfit are assigned to escort a sailor convicted of a crime up the coast to a military prison. This crime does need to be known to the audience, because it is so petty that it wins protagonist and audience sympathy. He had stolen seven dollars out of a church collection for a charity. He is a sad sack, a luckless, joyless personality with even worse luck because the charity is the favorite of the wife of one of the Top Brass. Quickly realizing that this young navy man has never known any pleasure in living, the protagonist (Nicholson) sets a goal of bringing fun into his life.

As they travel up the East Coast to military prison, the sad sack is treated to some of the pleasures of life. Revealing the petty nature of the theft is essential to show the luckless type of fellow he is. It makes the protagonist objective to cheer him up all the more understandable. It also plays strongly on audience sympathy both for the protagonist and his goal and for the hapless fellow who is treated to the joy of living for the first time in his life.

The motion picture *Deliverance* is discussed in Chapter 5 for its point-of-action opening that catches the men on the way to the river for their holiday trip. The audience knows nothing personal about these men and their backgrounds. But the exposition threading through the river ride provides information about them. For example, as the ride becomes rough, the boats bounding into the rapids, one of the men wonders that he left his happy home and good job for this. Exposition is the vehicle to put each of the men in sharper focus. However, for this type of story, only a minimal amount needs to be known concerning what happened before. The men bring no problems to the river trip; they start on the river as carefree vacationers. The situations that confront them explode into high melodrama.

Exposition in *Jaws* is a part of the sharp conflict between Police Chief Brody and the mayor. Out of the police chief's insistence on closing the beaches after the first shark killing and the mayor's refusal, the audience learns that this is a beach resort dependent on summer tourists. A shark scare would drive away their business, especially with the Fourth of July holiday approaching. Such exposition, vital to the story line, is woven into it in a natural way through conflict.

As well as opening on the point of action, "The Gift" (the episode of "The Waltons" discussed in Chapter 5) sets essential exposition with the cautioning by the young Seth's mother not to overstrain himself. He had been recently ill. With the Waltons, Seth, and his mother gathered around the table waiting to listen to the radio show, the viewer also learns that Seth's father is a country and western musician and that the boy wants to be a musician like his father. This opening scene is a skillful blending of point of action and the exposition—that which is essential in building the story.

Another effective and unusual use of exposition is in a return visit of Jean Stapleton as Edith in a episode of "Archie Bunker's Place." Jean Stapleton has endeared herself to millions of television viewers as Edith Bunker of "All in the Family" and has also won an Emmy and other awards for the role. But after years of playing Edith, Stapleton left the show. After the 1979–80 television season opened, she made a return visit. Although Stapleton's departure from the show was highly publicized, her absence in the earlier segments of "Archie Bunker's Place" needed explaining to the viewers to whom Edith had become an idol. The exposition in her first guest appearance serves a dual purpose, not only explaining the absence of Edith in previous segments of the new season, but also setting up the story—and at the action point, which opens the segment.

Edith confides a problem to Archie's business partner (played by Martin Balsam). She had a job working in a sanitarium but was fired. Now she is about to go out on an interview for a new job but is afraid to try again. However, she gains courage through the encouragement of Archie's partner and goes out for that interview. This scene combines exposition (explaining Edith's absence) and setting the basis for the strong conflict of the story line. Typical of Archie and his narrow views, he believes that a woman's place is in the home and opposes her taking a job. The conflict is resolved as his partner acts as mediator, persuading Archie to reconcile himself to Edith's working. Thus, Jean Stapleton's continuing absence from the show can be accounted for. However, the problem is resolved in the opening episode of the 1980–81 season. Edith has passed away, and the effective first segment of the new season has Archie wrestling with adjustment to her death, not wanting to face what has happened and finally allowing his true feelings to surface. Here too, exposition blended into the story line of the episode provides a vivid picture of the passing of Edith. Skillfully woven into the script as part of that plot line, exposition explains to the viewer what went before that episode began.

Remember to be adroit with exposition. Don't shovel in explanations of what went before, but blend them in as part of the story line as the script thrusts ahead.

DISASTER!

Generally, disaster films require twofold exposition: essential background for the major people involved and, often, background for a buildup to the actual disaster. In *The Poseidon Adventure,* the Stirling Silliphant and Wendell Mayes screenplay of the Paul Gallico novel, conflict is introduced early with the captain and the ship's company man arguing over the sailing course. The captain fears that the ship is sailing directly into the path of a tidal wave. Insisting that the schedule must be met, the company man refuses to allow the captain to turn back the ship.

In the scene following, as passengers are assembled at a New Year's Eve dinner celebration, important information about the major characters is threaded in. This is essential exposition that whips up audience interest in these characters before disaster strikes. The tidal wave then crashes in. By this time, the audience cares about what happens to these people.

Exposition is threaded in selectively. Everything important need not be revealed in the one scene. The audience is told what needs to become known at such times when the information is needed. For example, the passengers led by the protagonist (portrayed by Gene Hackman) are climbing up the overturned ship in an attempt to reach the hull, which is above water. A formidable obstacle to their arduous and perilous climb is the water that has flooded the section of ship that they have reached. The only way to know if there is an exit on the other side of the water is if someone can swim across. A middle-aged housewife (enacted by Shelley Winters) volunteers. A line of exposition here covers her reason for volunteering; if offered before, it would have seemed irrelevant to the film. It is likely, too, that audiences would have forgotten this information by the time it needed to be known in the film.

At this critical moment, she tells her fellow passengers that she won a swimming contest when she was sixteen. That information is essential to give credibility to the swim, and it is fitted in at the logical time—when it needs to be known. This is the moment when she has to persuade the others that she is capable of making the swim. If she had introduced her swimming prowess earlier, the comment would have appeared contrived and would likely have been forgotten by audiences much before the critical moment of its importance.

The Towering Inferno also traps a group of people in a disaster situation when they gather for a gala formal party in the tower of a newly constructed skyscraper superstructure. The screenplay, again by Stirling Silliphant and Wendell Mayes, skillfully blends the excitement of two original novels, *The Tower,* by Richard Martin Stern, and *The Glass Inferno,* by Frank M. Robinson.

The guests are already assembled, and the type of building and background of its construction are facts provided by exposition skillfully woven through the opening scenes, covering these essential details about which the audience needs to have information in order to understand what the film is about. By the time Ron MacAllister, protagonist, arrives by helicopter on the roof of the superstructure, the locale—San Francisco—has already been established through the visual excursion, as have the names of the building and company that owns it.

Greeted by James Duncan, the tycoon who owns it all, MacAllister is asked about his trip and whether he has changed his mind about quitting his job there and moving out of the city. But MacAllister hasn't. He tells Duncan that after the party that night, he will turn in his black tie and move out of the city. More points about MacAllister are threaded in as exposition while the story is advancing: MacAllister is quitting his job as chief architect of the building; he is moving out of San Francisco, and he is expected at a formal party held that night in the building. Note the reference to his black tie.

On his way to his office on the seventy-ninth floor, Will Giddings, the construction chief, runs excitedly to MacAllister and informs him of the failure of the dampers to open. MacAllister is puzzled. He thinks that the Thompson G-12 electromagnets that went into the dampers should work effectively. Giddings tells him that not G-12s, but G-4s, went into the dampers. The failure of the dampers at this time is not exposition, but story advancement.

However, something else happened before that. Before the motion picture opened—before the story got under way—Thompson G-4s went into the dampers. This error provides the potential for the fire that will engulf the building, and the explanation of the error that happened before is exposition.

In his office, MacAllister is greeted by his girlfriend, Susan, and the audience learns still more about him. The exposition is conveyed through conflict—argument over whether he should quit his job here. In opposition to such a move, Susan believes that their futures belong in San Francisco, his as an architect, hers as a managing editor. His dream is to build a town along the cliffs above the town of Mendocino. This is more exposition, just as exposition skillfully weaves in the background of some of the key party guests.

FLASHBACKS—BE QUICK

There are special times when flashbacks may be appropriate in exposition. The previous chapter discussed the handling of flashbacks in relating what went before the opening provocative point-of-action scene. But what about flashbacks purely as exposition? The answer is that flashbacks can only be a cluttering crutch if looked upon as the easiest way to fit in what went before the story opens. The need is to tell the story without the interruption of cutting back. Relying on a flashback instead of lacing in the exposition calls for sound skill. Today's pace in filmmaking also demands that you do not take too much time flashing back to what went before.

In this electronic age, the viewer's eyes and ears are tuned to quicker images. If flashbacks must be used in a script, the flashing image that tells in seconds what has gone before is the most expedient and effective filmmaking way.

The Pawnbroker, starring Rod Steiger, initiated this technique as the means of showing that the protagonist is haunted by a memory of a barbed wire fence. This fence, it is further disclosed, represents a Nazi concentration camp. The flashing image, recurring at pertinent moments, serves the story better than a thousand words. Another such use of the swift-image flashback is made in the movie *Midnight Cowboy,* in which the protagonist (portrayed by Jon Voight) believes he should be in great demand among the women of New York as a high-priced stud. The film opens at the point-of-action start of his bus ride from a small western town to the city.

On the bus his thoughts of his popularity with the girls back home are revealed in the quick-image flashback technique. This is exposition. Otherwise, the audience would not understand why he is so convinced that he is irresistible to women. But in cynical, sophisticated New York, women are not willing to pay for his stud services. Despite the rebukes, his persistent pursuit of his goal is all the more understandable because of other flashbacks that bear out his self-image. In particular, flashbacks of him as a boy with his grandmother show how she pampered him. By this technique, the audience is made to understand him and sympathize with his frustrations. The quick flashbacks do not interrupt the advance of the story line. Thus, without a moment's lag, the story builds its power. Dustin Hoffman also gives a fine performance as a cripple with whom the "Midnight Cowboy" shares his lodgings in the basement of a condemned building.

The flashbacks just described are the flashing type of images. Sound is not necessary to convey the exposition. But sometimes the quick image needs a voice accompaniment for the exposition to be understandable and effective. "A Matter of Life and Death," a teleplay by Albert Aley written for "Quincy," opens with Quincy driving in his own car (not an official coroner's vehicle) on a state highway. Obviously, he is out of town, away from his coroner's job. Why? Where is he going? Exposition through quick voice flashbacks provides the answers.

As Quincy drives, he is thinking of what happened that led to his leaving town. What happened is revealed in flashbacks. These are quick flashbacks with dialogue as well as images. Quincy's nerves are becoming strained. He upbraids Sam, his hardworking assistant in the lab, and argues with Monahan of the police force and, finally, with Astin, his boss. It is Astin's pointing out to Quincy his ill-tempered behavior caused by his dealing too long with the dead that has motivated Quincy to take this trip. Even as Quincy thinks back, the story is thrusting forward, for an accident occurs on the road as he drives. This becomes the major cause and major problem for Quincy, who becomes involved by taking over a small-town doctor's work while he is on vacation. Use of the voice flashback exposition while Quincy is driving moves the action directly into the story. It is a skillful blend.

Sometimes a flashback for exposition requires a little more in the way of a scene dramatization. The motion picture *Bless the Beasts and Children,* a Stanley Kramer production, tells the story of a group of boys together in a boys' camp with a strong objective—to save the buffalo.

By government order, a selected number are shot each year, and the boys cannot bear to let that happen. In the opening point-of-action scene they pretend that they are the buffalo and, one by one, drop "dead" in simulated shootings. The story is under way, and they are in action as they sneak out of the camp in early dawn to embark on their mission. It involves stealing a car for their long trip to their destination, and soon the police are seeking them. The head of the camp also reports them missing.

At this point the audience knows little about them except that they have sensitivity enough to want to save the buffalo and that they are looked upon as misfits by camp officials and the other boys in the camp. A fuller picture is needed, then, of why they are looked upon as misfits. What motivates them? What makes them tick?

One boy is leader of the group as protagonist, with the others allied with him. Since they are a misfit group with a single objective, the flashback into each of their lives illuminates the discord and conflict in their homes that result in the parental unloading of them on the camp and their being dubbed misfits. Each flashback represents what happened before the screenplay opens and so clearly is exposition, and each is deftly laced into the story as it moves ahead. There is no break in continuity.

It is not often that a script requires multiple scene flashbacks. But if this is so essential that you must use the scene dramatization, remember that such flashbacks must not stop the story or slow it, and they should blend into the body of the action.

You must be selective, too, in your flashbacks: Do not overdo. A story editor of one of the top-rated television shows said he could not read past two pages of one script submitted to him because the writer used a flashback almost every other line.

SKILLFULLY WOVEN EXPOSITION

Screenplays as well as the script intended for television should not be overburdened with an abundance of flashbacks. It is wiser to tell your story in progressive sequences, weaving in the exposition of what went before at the appropriate moments. Think of the musician's girlfriend in the "Columbo" script telling him that she knows he won't give up his wife because of her money. Think of the hard hat worker—so identified to the audience—jumping on the back of a truck and concertizing on a piano when both vehicles are stalled in traffic.

In the motion picture *Chinatown,* with an original screenplay by Robert Towne that won an Oscar, Evelyn Mulrey (played by Faye Dunaway) wants to hire private investigator Gittes (Jack Nicholson in the role) to find out the identity of the woman she suspects that her husband is seeing. Gittes tells her that he doesn't come cheap. Her reply is that money is no object to her. Thus, in one line of dialogue—one line of exposition—the screenplay sets her up as a woman of means. Through further questioning by Gittes, the audience also learns that her husband is chief engineer for the city's water and power department.

Later, when in pursuit of answers to what becomes a murder case (her husband is murdered), Gittes calls at the department and finds out that her father was founder and architect of the entire water system. Gittes further establishes that information by the father's portrait hanging on the wall along with other departmental chiefs. The investigation in a murder mystery offers a wealth of opportunities to weave in exposition—what went before—as the information needs to be revealed.

Whatever your selection of exposition, remember: You must not stop the forward thrust of your story because of the exposition. Your script must progress. Exposition will fit in as perfectly as the pieces of a completed jigsaw puzzle, and only you, the writer, will have been aware of how you fitted those pieces together. Even then, they will be fitted into your script in such a natural way that you will surprise yourself. Once you have your story worked out and the flow of continuity within your grasp, exposition will quite naturally be a part of it.

Now let's take a close look at the way to develop your motion picture or teleplay in order to sustain interest. To open your script at the point of action is essential. Your story must begin at the provocative point of the story you want to tell. Let's examine how you move ahead with it. How do you build your script so that it sustains interest throughout?

7

The Build

In the theater the popular question for the playwright hopeful of a production for his play and a successful run is "How's your second act?" The first act must capture strong interest in the protagonist and his problem, and the third act should offer a satisfactory resolution. Between the first and third acts is the core—the middle—continuing the build in order to sustain interest. This build reaches the highest suspense point, which becomes the point of no return for the protagonist—the point at which all seems lost. The antagonist's counterthrust has provided the most potent setback of any of the counterthrusts that have gone before.

The protagonist has been capable of answering each counterthrust with a thrust forward that keeps the play in a progressive stage—building and building. The curtain before the final one must leave the protagonist at the most critical point. If a play should find its way to production without building interest through the second act (unfortunately, too many do, making the difference between hits and failures), the theater will likely be emptied of both customers and critics.

The theory of "How's that second act?" play building also applies to the screenplay and teleplay. Although in the motion picture there are no act breaks, the pacing is the same. The sustaining of interest and increased momentum carries the script along to the peak of crisis and, then, the resolution. But since in television the act breaks define each phase of the build at a cliff-hanger point, with the highest point the act before the last, we select the television script as a guideline. The build of the one-hour show also applies to the long form (feature film) for television. As already pointed out, an effective screenplay also follows the build pattern, even though the continuity does not break into acts. For the screenplay to sustain interest it follows a similar pattern; this is how scripts build momentum and interest out of the suspense of what will happen next and if the protagonist will win out.

TIMING A ONE-HOUR TELEPLAY

In Act 1, the major characters must be introduced and set into action. The key problem must be established, i.e., the protagonist objective and the antagonist opposition—the hurtling of the obstacles. Because the protagonist is in trouble over the strong antagonist opposition, the first act ends in a cliff-hanger. There is a problem, and trouble.

The trouble mounts in Act 2. As the protagonist thrusts forward, the antagonist delivers the counterthrusts. The protagonist is an admirable character and is bright enough to circumvent those counterthrusts and move ahead once more. But the antagonist is always ready with another counterthrust. Trouble piles up. Act 2 ends with another cliff-hanger. It indicates that the script is moving toward its strongest crisis point.

The momentum builds. Act 3 takes the protagonist deeper and deeper into crisis. He is trying hard. But again and again the antagonist sets back the protagonist's thrusts ahead. That puts the protagonist in the worst possible trouble at the end of Act 3, with what appears to be no way out. The cliff-hanger is at its most suspenseful. Of course, the last act—Act 4 of the one-hour show—holds the resolution. In the longer forms, the same pattern of build prevails. The difference in television is the number of acts: five for the ninety-minute show and six for the two-hour show. Of course, the longer the show, the more act breaks. Those commercials pay for the cost of the show.

The timing of the acts of the one-hour-show is fairly uniform. The opening tease or hook has the shortest length, because within two or three minutes the viewer should be teased into continuing to watch. However, the total first act playing time is usually longer than for the rest of the acts because of the need to establish two important factors that form the foundation:

1. All the major characters must be introduced in the first act.

2. The major problem must be introduced, and the cross-conflict of protagonist versus antagonist must get well under way.

Establishing these key factors usually results in a longer first act. A playing time of from seventeen or eighteen to twenty minutes is the first act norm. Into the second act the tempo quickens. Once the cross-conflicts are well under way, the situations producing each set of thrust and counterthrust build in fhat quicker tempo. That pares the second act down to approximately fourteen or fifteen minutes. The third act, ending in the strongest of the act break cliff-hangers and building with increased momentum, usually plays approximately twelve minutes. Although exceptions may occur depending on the type of material, the one-hour show's timing pattern conforms to this timing.

TIMING OF OTHER FORMS

However, the longer forms do not establish that uniformity. For example, the third act may run fifteen minutes and the second, ten or twelve minutes. One theory for such variation is the ratings war. A viewer watching an hour show may want to sample another show during the commercial break. But the viewer who switches to another hour show will be likely to tune in on another commercial break because of the uniformity of the hour-long programming. However, a switch to a longer form, such as the two-hour, would possibly put the viewer right in the midst of an act. If that act holds enough interest, the viewer may abandon the one-hour show to stay with this two-hour one.

Of course, the way to hold viewer interest is with an interesting script that not only captures immediate attention, but sustains the suspense of wondering what will happen next—interest that should be sustained from scene to scene. Fundamentally, the excellent script provides a better chance of catching the story editor's interest and so making the sale.

The half-hour television show—generally a situation comedy—divides into two acts, with a crisis point for the protagonist where all appears lost. The second act overcomes the crisis and resolves the protagonist's problem. Playing time for each act is equally divided.

These are the basics of timing. Within that framework of the timing, and paraphrasing Shakespeare's "the play's the thing," the build is the thing that gives the script its life.

AN EFFECTIVE BUILD

What makes the effective build? The cross-conflicts of protagonist and antagonist—the thrusts and counterthrusts on a scale of rising action—build the interest and suspense. As the action continues on, the pattern of peaks and valleys builds to that most critical point for the protagonist.

When the protagonist moves ahead in a forward thrust, he is climbing toward a peak or goal—the objective he urgently wants—and he drops down when the antagonist strikes a counterthrust. It is like a mountain climb, with the protagonist trying to reach the summit and seeming to succeed just as a rock slide dislodges him. But he manages to save himself and resume the climb, climbing higher and also pushing back the antagonist. But another counterblow again sets him back, until he can regain his footing and advance again.

Figure 7-1 on page 98, illustrates the cross-conflicts of a story line that throws the protagonist action into the peaks and valleys of success and setbacks. At the same time, the antagonist pattern shapes into similar peaks and valleys, for as the protagonist advances, the antagonist is set back. This is a general pattern; it

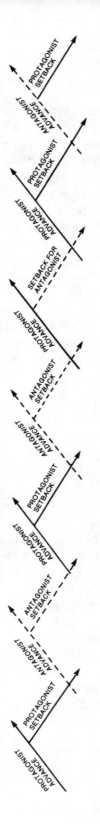

FIGURE 7-1. Antagonist's last advance on this graph. Next move for the antagonist sets protagonist back, producing crisis that seems to put protagonist at point of no return. Will protagonist ever get out of this?

does not specify any one teleplay or screenplay, but the general build to the crisis point—the protagonist point of no return.

Conversely, the antagonist advance signals a protagonist setback, but the crisis for the protagonist—that point of no return—is brought about only after the strongest of the antagonist counterthrusts.

From that crisis point the resolution is developed. The protagonist will find a way out of that worst predicament of all with a new thrust forward and, usually, another counterthrust by the antagonist that this time loses all force as the protagonist scores the victory.

For the continuation of Figure 7-1, see Figure 7-2 below.

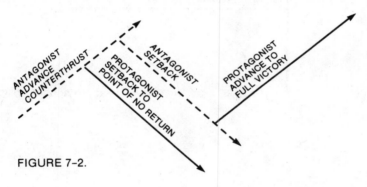

FIGURE 7-2.

SOME EXAMPLES

In the motion picture *The Getaway,* the antihero protagonist (portrayed by Steve McQueen) is put through the thrust and counterthrust paces and finally recovers his share of the money that had been stolen from him in a double cross. The money is loot from a robbery. This is a moment of near triumph. His last stop is a cheap hotel in a western town from which he intends to make a run across the border into Mexico with his wife and the fortune, small though it is. But the leader of the antagonist force and his associates plan to gun him down. They surround him, cutting off escape from the second floor hotel room. Their choking off his escape at gunpoint is the most cataclysmal threat of all.

But in the shoot-out, against the tremendous odds, he blasts his way out, and, with the money and his wife to help him enjoy the fortune, he happily crosses the border. For *The Getaway,* see Figures 7-3 and 7-4 below.

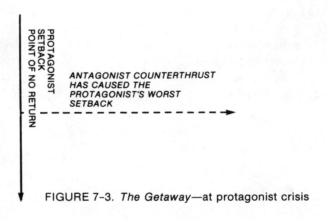

FIGURE 7-3. *The Getaway*—at protagonist crisis

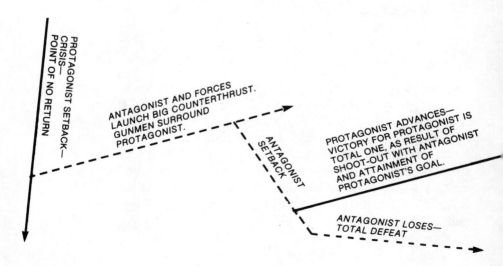

FIGURE 7-4. *The Getaway*—Will protagonist save himself?

Thrust and Counterthrust

Keep this in mind: Before the high peak of crisis which every script, motion picture or television, should reach, the peaks and valleys of thrust and counterthrust are building the momentum of rising action. On these crosscurrents, the protagonist advances in his thrust forward against the antagonist, only to be set back by the antagonist counterthrust. Conversely, a protagonist setback proves a winning move or advance for the antagonist, while a protagonist *advance* is an antagonist *setback*. This crosscurrent of thrust/counterthrust sustains the "What happens next?" interest. It is a good way also to check yourself on whether your script is building in an interesting way.

The expertly written *Dog Day Afternoon,* by Frank Pierson, stars Al Pacino as Sonny, the antihero protagonist. The movie takes Sonny through his ups and downs during a bank robbery he undertakes. With a great deal of suspense and excitement as well as humor, the action consistently swings from the advance moves of Sonny trying to escape to the counterthrusts of Detective Moretti and police he heads trying to capture Sonny. Sonny takes hostages in the bank, but only finds a small amount of money available to him. His aim then is to get out clear, but he encounters problems. Burning some papers of the bank register in a wastebasket creates smoke, which attracts outside attention. Soon police are drawn to what's going on in the bank. In a phone call to Sonny, Detective Moretti demands Sonny's surrender. Sonny's threat to throw his hostages' bodies out on the street causes Moretti to back off. However, Moretti has his counterthrust, and the police lay siege. Sonny is forced into releasing one live hostage, the bank guard. In locking horns with Moretti in negotiations for what he hopes is his escape, Sonny steps outside the bank to find that crowds have gathered on the street, cheering him wildly. He has almost a folk hero dimension. This gives him a sense of importance and confidence, and he demands that Moretti order his cops to put their guns down. His demand is obeyed, but Moretti orders the air conditioning in the bank turned off. This is another of Moretti's counterthrusts following advances made by Sonny in trying to attain his goal.

Sonny demands a jet to fly him out of the country with Sal. Early in the bank robbery, Jackie chickened out and Sonny allowed him to leave the bank—to walk away. This was before the police became aware of what was happening in the bank. But now the police are retaliating by turning off the air conditioning and with an attempt to break into the bank through the rear door. Sonny becomes alerted to this counterthrust in time to stop the break-in and also obtains from Moretti the promise of safe passage out of the country.

In the alternating of protagonist advances and antagonist counterthrusts, Sonny's request to see his wife is granted. This becomes another intriguing twist in the story line, with Leon as the wife in what is revealed as a homosexual relationship. The script builds in interest and suspense, with Moretti's trying to force Sonny's surrender through Leon. This is not accomplished. But although Sonny has that promise of a jet plane to fly him and Sal out of the country, along with the transportation to the plane—a strong advance for Sonny—Moretti has orders from the police commissioner to see that Sonny and Sal never get off the ground. This is strong counterthrust. It is a crisis point, and it looks like the point of no return.

Then Sonny and Sal are in the limousine en route to the airport and the waiting jet. Sonny appears to have won the next round. He and Sal have refused to relinquish their rifles, and the hostages are with them as their safety valve. Sonny has also won a skirmish with Sheldon, the FBI man in charge now, to have the driver changed to one he thought he could trust better.

At this stage, the protagonist fortunes have risen to the peak, while the antagonist aim to prevent escape has been thwarted. With escape at hand for Sonny and Sal, the screenplay thrusts forward into high gear—protagonist advance that appears to become total protagonist triumph. But suddenly, everything changes. Sonny is betrayed. As they reach the airport and are to transfer from the limousine to the waiting jet, Sheldon grabs Sonny's rifle in swift action, and the driver levels a gun at Sal. Before Sal can fire his rifle, he is shot to death.

Sonny is put under arrest. The hostages all go free. It's all over. It's that type of story, based upon a true happening in

Brooklyn, New York, which Frank Pierson fashioned into his excellent screenplay. The Build of the screenplay is highly effective in the handling of the thrusts and counterthrusts—protagonist advances, antagonist setbacks. Suspense was sustained throughout. No scene repeats itself, nor should a repetitive scene be a part of any effective script. Characters should act in a progression of crosscurrents to that crisis point of no return for the protagonist, and then the resolution. Note, too, that before that worst point for the protagonist, he thinks he is attaining success in accomplishing his purpose. As soon as Sonny is on his way to the airport with Sal, he is elated. He and Sal both breathe sighs of relief. But the tables turn. The force and speed of the counterthrust causes the death of Sal and the capture of Sonny.

Luke Skywalker must overcome tremendous odds in *Star Wars*. All through this superb science fiction motion picture, excitement is sustained in thrilling, edge-of-the-seat successions of thrusts and counterthrusts until the forthright, courageous Luke—with his stalwart friend Han Solo assisting him—wins over the onslaught of the enemy spaceships commanded by the Death Star as lead ship, gunning his spaceship to final victory. Not one moment lags in this science fiction action epic that is also richly imaginative in characterizations.

A FEW EXCEPTIONS

Two motion pictures that have proven to be great box office successes do not measure up as presentations of the most effective types of screenplays: *Superman* and *Close Encounters of the Third Kind*. *Superman* has attracted tremendous audiences everywhere: Superman, the character, is a built-in attraction. But Clark Kent does not make his famous fast-change transformation into Superman until well into the movie. Viewers cheer at the sight of Superman zooming out to prevent a disabled helicopter from crashing and in so doing, rescuing the lone passenger, Lois Lane. At last, here's Superman! The sight of Superman relieves a large amount of frustration—mass audience frustration—over having to wait so long before Superman zooms onto the screen. A lesser attraction than Superman likely would not have the good fortune to offset a screenplay that lags in spots.

Let's look more closely. Christopher Reeve in a fine performance as the great Superman is a considerable asset. Sent to Earth in a space capsule by his father to escape the explosion of his native planet, Krypton, Superman is taken through the paces from babyhood through growing up, is cared for by foster parents on their farm, and in young manhood ventures to Metropolis and obtains a news reporter job on the *Daily Planet.* Meanwhile, a great deal of footage is consumed, while audiences sit through more than a quarter of the movie to wait for that first sight of Superman.

This is too long to wait because the story of Superman in action—the story of Superman versus the formidable antagonist Lex Luthor, played by Gene Hackman—does not begin until after Superman's first action to save the helicopter. The sequences of Superman's growing up and gaining his superstrength contain small peaks and valleys—small problems encountered and surmounted—but they lack the grappling of the main event, Superman versus the superantagonist.

The transformation of Clark Kent into Superman is too long delayed, thus deferring any suggestion that the story line is going to shape up with a Superman versus Luthor main plot line. A mugger accosts Clark Kent and Lois at gunpoint. But with Clark the mild-mannered fellow, it is Lois who takes action and kicks the mugger who, when he tumbles to the pavement, is still able to grip his gun and fire at Clark. Kent drops to the ground, but only with a slight hand injury—fortunately for him, and fortunately for the audience. He has his whole life ahead, with Superman a major part of it. This scene that has the mugger running away is lightly humorous because it is the girl who takes action against the mugger, not Clark Kent. In his encounter with the mugger, Clark Kent was knocked down. He was at least spared a complete knockout, but he sat, appearing dazed, against a wall. Not until Clark Kent changes into Superman and saves Lois Lane and the helicopter is the Man of Steel (finally) visible, demonstrating strength and flying speed.

However, his superaction does not advance the story line or represent any element of it any more than the scene involving the mugger. Superman's escort of Lois Lane on a night flight over Metropolis has charm and humor in it. But that, too, is an incident that is separate from the main story line. The story that should be the heart of the action-adventure has not been introduced yet. Besides, when audiences do meet Lex Luthor, it is not through any employment of Superman wit and super-strength. The police want Luthor, that arch-criminal, and two cops, spotting Otis (Luthor's henchman) in Metropolitan Station (the equivalent of New York's Grand Central), start to give chase. However, they lose the trail along the tracks after Otis jumps into an indentation on one and disappears. But Otis' devious route leads him to his intended destination—the head-quarters of his boss, the master-criminal Luthor. It is then that Luthor speaks of his Crime of the Century that he will put into operation. But a Superman crosscurrent meeting with Luthor does not occur until later. It is then that Superman and the audience learn of Luthor's violently explosive scheme to increase the value of his real estate holdings in Nevada by destroying California.

Even then Superman does not have a strong confrontation with Luthor that sets him into action against him. The super-cleverness that should give a Superman—in fact, any Superhero—the ability to get himself on the trail of the arch-criminal and discover the diabolical plot is lacking. Even when Superman and Luthor have a confrontation—and not too strong a one—setting Superman into action against the archvillain, Superman and Luthor do not engage in crosscurrent protagonist-versus-antagonist moves.

The action should follow a pattern of protagonist advance and antagonist counterthrust, representing the crosscurrents of conflict in rising action. (See Figure 7-5, page 106.)

The strong, suspenseful crossconflict pattern should continue until Superman wins total victory. Instead, this pattern is dominant:

PROTAGONIST

ANTAGONIST

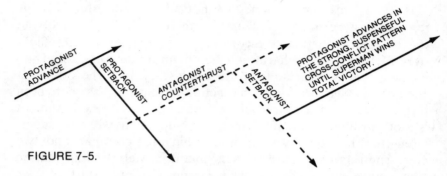

FIGURE 7–5.

The progatonist and antagonist are each on an independent course.

Not until Luthor activates his monstrous land-exploding plan does the movie show any story line vitality. But it still does not build to the suspense and excitement that crosscurrent thrusts and counterthrusts would produce.

Superman's multiple circling of the globe is still a solo flight. Despite the whirlwind visual action, it is still a Superman solo flight that lacks the suspense and excitement that would have been generated if Superman and Luthor locked horns in the crosscurrents of mortal conflict. They are still operating on separate wavelengths:

PROTAGONIST

and

ANTAGONIST

What is missing is not only the suspense of advance and setback for each side, but the fight-to-the-finish between Superman and Luthor. A final confrontation with Luthor—a strong fight-to-the-finish before he captures the archvillain—is omitted. The demand for the highest peak of suspense in the trapping of Luthor is ignored.

There is a new flurry of excitement after Superman's circling the globe to foil Luthor's superplot. This occurs when Superman returns to Luthor's headquarters—undoubtedly to take care of the last piece of business—and rescues Eve (who is Luthor's ladyfriend and the target, too, for his villainies) from her suspension on the feeding hook where she dangles over the monster pit. Superman then turns his attention to Otis and, obviously, to his intention of capturing Luthor, too.

But here, too, after that one new stir of excitement, the script flattens out. Figure 7-6 continues with Superman on a plateau from the scene in Luthor's hideout to Superman's capture of Otis and Luthor.

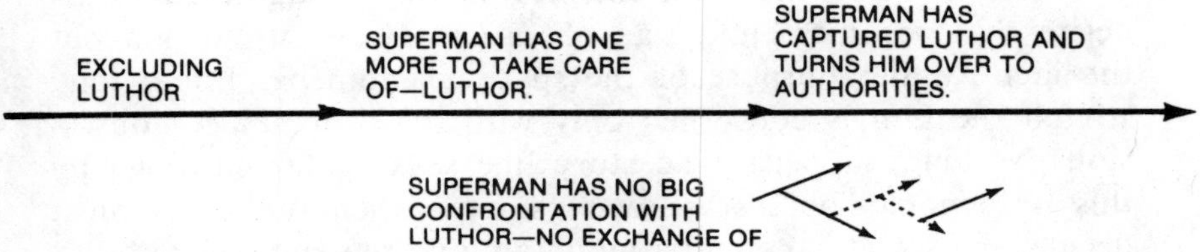

FIGURE 7-6. Superman (protagonist) round-up of crime ring

However, there has been no counterthrust leading to the capture, none of the hair-raising, spine-tingling fight-to-the-finish action that should make for a resounding finale. Instead, Superman delivers Luthor and Otis to the authorities. This is after-the-fact. Luthor has already been captured. What should have been enacted excitingly becomes a behind-the-scenes *fait accompli,* and, therefore, an all too tame capping of Superman's total victory. If the story buildup had intensified, Luthor could have further exercised his cunning in attempts to outwit Superman, because he would have been pitted more frequently against the fabulous Man of Steel. Superman could have then displayed his superstrength; he could call upon his cleverness to stop Luthor's counterthrust.

The motion picture is a box office success. But without the tremendous mass appeal of Superman, the failure to tell a consistently suspenseful story would have given it less appeal. Don't gamble on a script that does not build steadily with the crosscurrents of conflict. In all probability you won't have the powerful, mass audience appeal of a Superman in your script to carry your work to full fruition on the screen. The writing of the script with an established (and in this case, spectacular) character name is generally assigned to the established writer with a track record. But whatever the case, write the best you can. Don't rely on any built-in props.

The original *Close Encounters of the Third Kind,* written and directed by Steven Spielberg, is a motion picture swept along to great box office success with a script that has an intriguing beginning and a stunning finale. The highly provocative beginning points to something out there in space disturbingly close to Earth, and the spectacular effects catch immediate interest. However, the film then concentrates on the protagonist and his desire that becomes almost an obsession: He wants to find out the identity and purpose of the space phenomena. For a long stretch the film is concerned only with the protagonist's obsession. Nothing happens. The story line sags, weighted down by this obsession. The story advances late, when the protagonist decides the secret is behind a mountain and sets out to climb it.

Accompanying him in his endeavor is a woman companion looking for her little boy who has disappeared. No conflict is attached to that, however, nor is the protagonist's wife's protest over his obsession a major conflict. In fact, she is dropped from the story when he starts out on the climb. This gives him a thrust ahead—the advance—and a counterthrust as the military tries to block his attaining his goal and finding out the secret of the spaceship. (See Figure 7-7 on page 109.) But he is allowed the forward step—the advance—and witnesses, with the theater audience, a spectacular event. The movie climaxes in the landing of that wondrous spacecraft and the World War II crew's disembarking from it. Along with the landing is the suggestion of friendliness in outer space: A traveler aboard that spacecraft offers a gesture of friendship.

This is intriguing and provides an answer that is quite satisfying. The protagonist has found out the secret of the spacecraft, and the friendly wave of one of the space creatures offers a forecast of friendly beings on other planets. But the suspenseful buildup of the film is lacking. The only opposition to the protagonist's thrust ahead in his search for answers is the military, when he comes near to finding out "what lies beyond." The prolonged, sagging middle of the script spoils any chance of a tense, suspenseful buildup that protagonist versus antagonist in terms of protagonist advance and the opposition counterthrusts would create and sustain with ever-heightening interest.

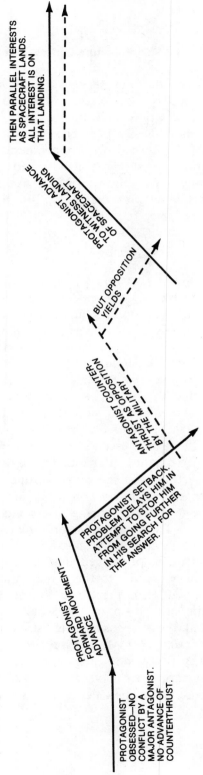

THEN PARALLEL INTERESTS AS SPACECRAFT LANDS. ALL INTEREST IS ON THAT LANDING.

PROTAGONIST ADVANCE TO WITNESS LANDING OF SPACECRAFT

BUT OPPOSITION YIELDS

ANTAGONIST OPPOSITION THRUST AS COUNTER-ADVANCE BY THE MILITARY

PROTAGONIST SETBACK. PROBLEM DELAYS HIM IN ATTEMPT TO STOP HIM FROM GOING FURTHER IN HIS SEARCH FOR THE ANSWER.

PROTAGONIST MOVEMENT— FORWARD ADVANCE

PROTAGONIST OBSESSED—NO CONFLICT BY A MAJOR ANTAGONIST. NO ADVANCE OF COUNTERTHRUST.

FIGURE 7-7.

Therefore, this film should not serve as your model for a tightly structured screenplay. Its success is based largely on special effects, and a new writer without the credits or achievement of a Spielberg cannot possibly get the picture budget such a spectacular demands. It must also be remembered that Spielberg is a highly acclaimed director who envisioned those effects. What he wrote is really a director's script. It has flaws in the build, in the structural quality of the build. But the spaceship landing in itself is remarkable.

THE OPEN SHOW

Clint Eastwood's *Play Misty for Me,* a motion picture he wrote, directed, and starred in, is a modestly budgeted picture. For the story it tells it needs no spectacular effects, but builds suspense through the thrust and counterthrusts of the protagonist hounded by a psychotic young woman obsessed by her mad love for him. His attempts to elude her are futile, and he turns to the police for help. The suspense builds.

Finally, it appears that the police have captured the woman. From a mounting cross-conflict, the conflict subsides, as shown in Figure 7-8 on page 111. The reason for suspension of conflict at this point is that after the crescendo of a suspenseful build, the script settles on a romantic plateau. The last protagonist forward thrust is the victory over the psychotic individual. With her out of his life, he settles into a romantic interlude with a new and normal young woman. During this romantic period, there is no counterthrust. The story line is on a plateau.

As you can see, no matter how pleasantly romantic the interlude, a plateau cannot be prolonged. The cross-conflict must be restored, building suspensefully to the climax and the resolution. When the obsessed female returns to the script, even though you are again caught up in the story's tension, you appreciate the fact that the suspense-thriller story line has not been abandoned. *Play Misty for Me* is a very satisfying motion picture, saved in time by Eastwood's judgment as a director.

As you can see, the scripts we have discussed for their story build are of the suspense type. The chief reason is that the cross-

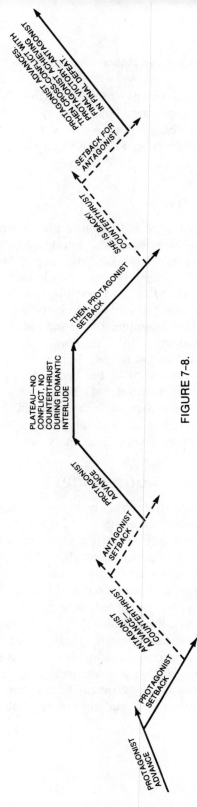

FIGURE 7-8.

conflicts stand out so sharply in these scripts that they are easy to follow. They are the "open show" types, where the antagonist—usually the criminal—is known from the start, and you follow his machinations and are eager for the protagonist to catch up with him.

THE CLOSED SHOW

The "closed show" type is the whodunit in which the crime is committed, but the identity of the antagonist or criminal is not known until the case is solved. Suspense is derived from the bouncing of suspicion among various characters who, one by one, are revealed to have motives for committing the crime. Surprise twists in the balancing of suspicions keep the story build interesting. For example, the protagonist is about to zero in on a prime suspect, only to find the quarry murdered. Nothing is what it seems to be, but everything needs to be credible. Red herrings should be avoided; i.e., the deliberate pointing of suspicion without real substance at a character to add more interest to the whodunit aspect is unfair to the audience, who will resent it. The false clue is as much a breach of buildup as any other diversion in the story line.

REMINDERS FOR A GOOD SCRIPT

A deadline injected into your script—a life-and-death deadline for the protagonist to race against and win out over—is a strong asset. However, the deadline must be believable and fit naturally in the script, or not be employed at all.

The elements of cross-conflict are basic to the build of any script. If the thrusts and counterthrusts build progressively (as they should in a well-constructed, interest-sustaining script), the momentum will carry the action to the climactic point, with the protagonist in the worst possible predicament. Remember that this occurs after the protagonist appears to have surmounted all obstacles and, along with the audience, senses total victory. (Of course, if there *were* total victory at that point, the show would not only be over, but the audience would be deprived of the thrills and spills of an interesting teleplay or screenplay.)

Recognize, too, that no two scenes will repeat themselves in the well-constructed script. Characters will have progressed in their actions so that they could not possibly repeat the scene.

THE BUILD IN COMEDY AND DRAMA

These elements are as essential to comedy and drama as to the suspense-thriller. Television's "Love Boat" illustrates the suspense ingredient inherent in each of the three complete stories that make up each week's one-hour segment. In "The Big Deal," by James F. Henry, the protagonist Alison, an attractive young woman, is a cruise passenger with her father, who needs to merge his company with another or face financial trouble. Brad, the man her father hopes will sign the merger contract, is also on the cruise.

Brad shows an immediate interest in Alison. But Alison and Jim meet aboard ship. Jim is a boyfriend from their high school days and musician whose dance band is playing this cruise. Their interest in each other is rekindled. Every step of the build-up of new romance with Jim receives a counterthrust through Brad's demands on Alison's time and interest. Alison cannot slight Brad, lest he cool off on the prospective merger contract with her father.

The crisis is reached after she makes a date with Jim and stands him up in order to go ashore with Brad. In love with her, Jim cannot accept her being nice to Brad, even if it's only to help her father. Although she loves Jim, she cannot refuse Brad's attentions and so wreck her father's business opportunity. Jim breaks up with her.

This is crisis time—the worst of all possible setbacks for Alison, for her main objective is winning Jim. Because her father's financial interests are also at stake, Brad, whose attentions she is forced to accept, is the stumbling-block antagonist. Now the viewer's interest is further quickened. The big question is, Will Alison and Jim reconcile? If they do, what will happen to the business merger—and her father? Of course, this is romantic comedy, so everything is resolved happily.

Keep in mind that this segment takes no more than twenty minutes' playing time. However, the elements of cross-conflict—advance moves and setbacks on each side—building to the most hopeless point in Alison's romance with Jim (the major theme) are the same as in any longer work of a more serious nature.

"Love, American Style," a long-run television show still seen in syndication reruns, includes short sketches in each segment (blackouts), some of which are no more than seven or eight minutes long. The difference between the short sketches and the longer-length shows is that the short forms leap into the problem much sooner. The tease problem/conflict is set up in moments. Every second is precious.

One sketch, written by Arnold Margolies, has a young man eloping. But he climbs into the second story room of the wrong house and becomes instantly involved with the wrong girl. Conflict and the crisis point occurs when his fiancée indignantly discovers his error. The windup has him marrying the wrong girl (who is now the right one). All of this takes place in only eight minutes.

North Dallas Forty (the movie written by Frank Yablans, Ted Kotcheff, and Peter Gent, adapted from the novel of that name by Peter Gent) has the football player protagonist in intense conflict with the crass commercialism of the game as represented by the team's owner. Finally, the protagonist reaches a peak point of triumph in his battle with the team's owner. He is to play in the big game. Suddenly, however, the team head's last minute reverse decision keeps him out of the game. This plunges him into a most critical setback.

However, the much-abused, long-suffering player kicks back, figuratively rear-ending the owner with a solid boot. He quits, walking out on the game to which he has dedicated himself, and that constitutes a moral victory. The girl friend who has opposed his suffering bruises in playing commercial football will also be pleased with his decision. His moral victory will bring personal happiness as well. Indeed, the long-suffering player experiences the final triumph. He has advanced, while the antagonist has lost a valuable football player and received a solid rejection from him.

CHECK YOURSELF

Keep in mind that the protagonist advance is an antagonist setback. This crosscurrent of thrust/counterthrust sustains the "What happens next?" interest. On the basis of thrust and counterthrust, advance and setback, you can check yourself on whether your script is building in an interesting way.

You may want to keep a master sheet before you as you watch television and jot down the progression of each scene. You can do the same for whatever movies you catch on television.

Remember: In all your writing, whether for television or motion picture, the basic ingredients of a well-written teleplay and screenplay are similar for sustaining interest. If a protagonist succeeds in scene after scene and the opposition is offering little or no counterthrust, viewer interest will flag. The antagonist is not formidable enough, and the protagonist will win all. On the other hand, if the antagonist enjoys successive successful counterthrusts, the script will also become static. The script will lack conflict, and the suspense that should keep building as protagonist forward thrusts—the advances—are blocked by antagonist counterthrusts will be missing.

ANALYSIS OF AN ACTUAL TELEPLAY

Let us trace the forward moves and setbacks of a protagonist in the teleplay "Uninvited Peril" by Robert Sherman for "Barnaby Jones."* Skillful writing maintains the interest, and how the protagonist advances and is set back builds the story, the momentum of the action.

In the provocative opening scene, a doting, obsessed mother, Verna, wants to save her son Duane from being apprehended by police. He's killed a girl, a bar pickup he brought up to his cheap one bedroom apartment. He asks his mother what he should do. He doesn't want to go back to what is looked upon as "that awful place." Verna advises him to get the body out of

*References to UNINVITED PERIL by Robert Sherman from the series BARNABY JONES are by permission of QM Productions. Copyright © 1979 QM Productions All Rights Reserved

there and hide it, then return to his room—he is in Los Angeles—and wait for her and her husband Stewart (Duane's stepfather) to arrive from Denver.

Betty Jones, protagonist, secretary to and daughter-in-law of private investigator Barnaby Jones, has not yet been introduced. Since all advances and setbacks will be considered from the protagonist point of view, this scene, establishing the commission of a crime, is the obligatory one for a script that is an open show. Remember, the open show is one in which the identity of the criminal is known.

In the next scene Verna is at Barnaby's office with Stewart because Duane is missing. When they arrived at his hotel, they learned that he had checked out, leaving no forwarding address. Verna wants to hire Barnaby to find her son. But Barnaby is out on a case with his associate, J. R. Besides, he does not handle missing person cases. But Betty can take the case and does, eagerly. She knows nothing about Duane's criminality—that he has murdered last night or that he has escaped from the mental institution after commission of an earlier crime. Verna knows that the alias Duane is using is Richard Davis, and she furnishes Betty that name. As her first lead, Betty learns that Richard Davis has worked at carpentry.

For Betty, the protagonist, whose primary objective is to find Duane, the first action on the case is—
ADVANCE

Now again, keep in mind that all advances and setbacks are from the protagonist's point of view—Betty's.

But at a lumberyard where Duane has been working, he is trying to collect his back-pay, and, obviously, once he is paid, he will continue his flight. Betty's efforts to find him can then be made more difficult. In a sense this is—
SETBACK

However, Betty has a lead that sets her checking lumberyards, phoning inquiries whether Duane is an employee at any of them. Her lead to lumberyards provides her with—
ADVANCE

But Verna and Stewart present themselves at Betty's apartment and become her uninvited overnight guests. Still, Betty is hopefully intent on finding Duane and goes to the office in early morning to her work. But Verna has picked up her newspaper, which Betty has not seen. A police drawing resembling Duane stares up at Verna. The body of a girl has been found in a ravine, from where a witness caught sight of a fleeing man, thus far unidentified. From the witness's description, a police artist sketched the suspect. This pushes Verna to make the threat that she will kill anyone who stands in her way. Although the threat is not known to Betty, the possibility of her becoming imperiled is posed. Of course, the viewer does not know that the threat will result in a dire predicament for Betty. But it does show the desperado tactics of antagonist Verna. From the protagonist point of view it is—

SETBACK

That the strong threat was made at the end of Act 1 also provides a cliff-hanger into Act 2. The cliff-hanger is essential to insure that the home viewer will wait through the commercial to find out what happens next.

In the opening of Act 2, at the office, Betty's phone calls have proved fruitful. She locates the lumberyard where Duane worked, obtains the information when he will be back for his paycheck and the address. Pleased at her progress in the case, Betty phones Verna at her apartment and relays the information to her. Verna and Stewart have rented a car and will start right out to the lumberyard. Since Betty's office is closer, she will drive there, arriving earlier than Verna and Stewart, and will have Richard wait for them. This progress for Betty in the case which she thinks is reaching a happy conclusion is—

ADVANCE

Returning to the lumberyard, Duane asks Winchell, the employer, for his paycheck. As he prepares the receipt for it, Winchell notices the morning newspaper on his desk and the police drawing of the murder suspect. Recognizing Duane (Richard Davis) as the man in the sketch, he is about to call the police on his phone in a back room when Duane stops him with a gun. As Betty comes in, Winchell shouts to her that Duane is wanted for murder. They fight, and Winchell knocks the gun from Duane's hand. As Duane retaliates by slamming a piece of lumber down on Winchell's head and knocking him out, Winchell is able to get off a shot at him. Still on his feet and gun in hand, Duane forces Betty outside and into her car. He orders her to drive. For Betty, this is—

SETBACK

Duane becomes semiconscious, slumping in the car seat. However, fearful of rousing him, Betty does not attempt to take the gun from his hand but to get out of the car. Her escape move is—

ADVANCE

However, Verna and Stewart drive up, and seeing what happened to Duane, Verna gets his gun and turns it on Betty. She has also stopped Betty from calling an ambulance for Duane. This is outright action threat to Betty. She is in great peril. The act ends here with a cliff-hanger of increasing intensity. For Betty it is—

SETBACK

An investigation has begun because Betty's car has been found abandoned with blood on the seat next to the driver's. Barnaby and J. R. have been called by Police Lieutenant Biddle to the scene. Deeply concerned that something has happened to Betty, Barnaby intends to go back to the office and look through her notes. He knows she was trying to locate a missing son for some people. Because an investigation is under way directed at helping Betty, the scene represents for Betty—

ADVANCE

In a stop at a hopsital, Verna gets a doctor outside to look at Duane, but refusing to let Duane be taken care of in the hospital, she orders the doctor at gunpoint into the car and to drive to his private office to treat her son. More deeply enmeshed, also captive in the car, Betty's trouble increases. For her—

SETBACK

At his office Barnaby's investigation of what happened to Betty builds. Her notes lead to his call to Winchell's lumberyard and to the story of the shooting. The clues to what happened to Betty add up when J. R. sees the police drawing in the paper of the hunted murderer who matches the picture in Betty's notebook of the man Verna hired her to locate. (Verna had shown her a picture of Duane.) The investigation points to hope for Betty, and so is—

ADVANCE

In the doctor's private office the doctor is extracting the bullet from Duane while Verna hovers nearby. Taking advantage of the preoccupation of Verna and Stewart with Duane, Betty dashes out the rear end only to be found by Stewart, who brings her back to the office at gunpoint, and peril for her that points to certain death. At this point of no return for Betty—

SETBACK

And another cliff-hanger act break.

In the opening scene of Act 4. Lieutenant Biddle phones in to Barnaby the information that the police drawing of the murderer has identified him as an escapee from the hospital for the criminally insane and that his mother had tried to help him escape some months before, for which she was given a suspended sentence. Reading a further clue to Betty in this, Barnaby studies a city map.

The further investigation is a "plus" for Betty. At least someone is working for her. And so—

ADVANCE

Betty's plight as prisoner is worsened because she is now tied up. But she is attempting to cut the tape binding her wrist on the edge of a chrome table. This implies some—

ADVANCE

In the meantime, Duane's condition is worsening; he is bleeding internally. But although the attention of Verna and Stewart is on Duane, Stewart is looking at Betty as the scene ends. Because of the possibility that he might discover that Betty is trying to get free, her attempt to free herself now holds for her the possibility of—

MORE SETBACK

In his office Barnaby, checking hospitals in the vicinity of where Betty's car was found, learns that Dr. Oxford disappeared after stepping outside the hospital with a woman who had inquired whether he had an office away from the hospital where he treated patients. Barnaby gets Dr. Oxford's home-office address. Because Barnaby is moving forward in his investigation—in possession of an important lead, this constitutes—

ADVANCE

At the doctor's office Betty succeeds in freeing her wrists and getting the gun from Verna. But Verna snatches up another weapon, a long scissors with which she lunges at Betty, certain that Betty won't be able to shoot her—certain that Betty cannot and won't pull the trigger. Betty's conflict and hesitation for that moment creates for her—

SETBACK

But Barnaby and J. R. break into the office and wrest the scissors from Verna, thus capturing both Verna and Stewart. Meanwhile, Duane has died. The doctor could not save him. The rescue of Betty and capture of the criminals constitute the final—

ADVANCE

A "tag" scene—the epilogue in Barnaby's office—has Barnaby pose the question to Betty whether she would have pulled the trigger, and she answers. She realizes that she would have had to pull the trigger.

This scene is an epilogue. Since the problem in the script has already been resolved, there is no advance or setback in regard to protagonist Betty. But it does tell the viewer that if Barnaby had not arrived in time, Betty would have acted to save herself. This is in keeping with the courage and quick thinking that is a part of Betty's personality and is necessary for the series. The home viewer must continue to think of Betty in admirable terms. The scene ends with a light touch and laughter concerning the expensive restaurant J. R. has selected for their dining that night—and the banter over who is paying.

You have seen graphically how this breakdown of the build of a television script points up the thrusts and counterthrusts, and their effects in advances and setbacks for the protagonist. It also illustrates how each act builds to a cliff-hanger act end, a basic feature of television scripts.

As an additional aid, the actual shooting script of "Uninvited Peril" is reprinted here, starting on the next page.

"Uninvited Peril" by Robert Sherman

ACT ONE

FADE IN:

1   EXT. APARTMENT HOUSE - ESTABLISH - NIGHT (STOCK)   1

An aging structure near MacArthur Park.

2   INT. CHEAP ONE BEDROOM APARTMENT - NIGHT   2

From outside, a flashing neon rhythmically invades the
darkness. DUANE PIERSON, 22, sits on the edge of the
rumpled bed wringing his hands. He stirs, turns on
the table lamp and we SEE he is wearing only faded
blue jeans, his tight lean body glistening with sweat
as he stares indecisively at the telephone. Fighting
back the urge to make the call, he rises to the mirror
and dabs a cloth at the blood trickling from scratch
marks that trail across his pale, boyishly handsome
face. Fear mounting, no longer able to postpone the
inevitable, he returns to the edge of the bed, braces
himself and dials for the operator. (DIRECTOR: Please
allow 30 feet for any dialogue or necessary action.)

                    DUANE
          Operator... I have to call Mrs.
          Verna Compton in Denver, Colorado
          ... collect...

3   INT. THE COMPTON BEDROOM - NIGHT   3

The PHONE RINGS. A hand reaches out from under a
quilted blanket, switches on the lamp and fumbles for
the pair of steel rimmed reading glasses lying next to
a digital clock that tells us it is 1:10 AM. Putting
on the glasses is STEWART COMPTON, 45, a carpenter,
sober, colorless as the faded pajamas he wears. As
he squints at the clock, the figure in bed beside him
stirs. Wearing a plastic cap to protect her hair
which is done up in large curlers, is his wife,
VERNA, 48.

                    VERNA
          Stewart, if that's one of the
          ladies at the health spa, tell
          her I can take her any time
          between three and five...

                                        (CONTINUED)

She mutters through a yawn, not reaching for the phone
even though it's on her side of the bed. Vain,
haughty, a physically powerful woman who can beguile
with down-home charm as easily as she can be blunt and
ruthless when it serves her purpose, Verna totally
dominates her emotionally fragile husband.

                    STEWART
          It's one o'clock, Verna. Nobody'd
          be calling for a masseuse this
          time of night...

He grumps as he shuffles around the bed, slapping at
the chill attacking his arms, and picks up the phone.

                    STEWART
                 (continuing)
          Hello...
                 (listens)
          Collect from where?
                 (listens; then to
                  wife)
          Verna... you know anyone in
          Los Angeles named Richard Davis?

                    VERNA
          Davis...?

INTERCUT DUANE AS NEEDED:

                    DUANE
                 (interrupting)
          Stewart, it's me... Me — !

Jolted, Stewart clasps his hand over the phone:

                    STEWART
          Verna — it's Duane!

She sits bolt upright in the bed, grabs the phone.

                    VERNA
          Hello... hello... It's all
          right, operator. I'll accept
          the call...
                 (beat)
          Duane... it's really you — ?

                    DUANE
          You're not going to have one of
          those spells, are you, Mother?
          Don't get excited.

                                    (CONTINUED)

122

                              VERNA
          Excited — ?
                    (to Stewart)
          My pill, my pills!
                    (to Duane)
          Dear child, how thoughtless can
          you be? Do you realize it's
          been almost four months since
          you broke out —
                    (catches herself)
          — since you got out of that
          awful hospital, and all the
          consideration you've shown your
          poor mother is one tacky postcard
          from San Francisco?!
                    (at pills Stewart
                     hands her)
          I'm not about to swallow this
          with my own spit, am I?!

                              DUANE
          I needed time to think things
          out. But I was going to get in
          touch with you...

                              VERNA
          After I was in my grave, no doubt.

                              DUANE
          I had to try and get my head
          together, Ma; make sense out of
          things. I even got myself a job
          after I hitched down here to L.A....
                    (beat)
          Then... I met this girl...

Verna tenses, drinks the pill down with the water
Stewart has fetched for her:

                              VERNA
          I knew it! That's why you forgot
          I even existed; Son, haven't I
          always warned you about pickups?
          Tramps, that's all they are.

He looks down at something and shudders:

                              DUANE
          That's why I called. I need
          your help... like before...

                                        (CONTINUED)

CONTINUED: (3)

                              VERNA
                     (suddenly apprehensive)
              Like before? — What is it,
              Duane? What's wrong?

                              DUANE
              It... it happened again, Mama.

DUANE'S POV

of the tousled blond hair on the head of a dead
girl, her outstretched arm lying limp and motionless
on the floor. If she is nude, we cannot tell because
the rest of her body is hidden behind the foot of the
bed.

RESUME INTERCUTTING

                              VERNA
              Oh, my Lord.

                              STEWART
              What is it?

                              VERNA
              Are you sure, Duane? Are you
              sure?

                              DUANE
              Yes. But I couldn't help myself.
              She was like that other girl:
              filth.

                              VERNA
              Shhhhh... Your mother understands.
              Now you just calm yourself...

                              DUANE
              Help me, Mama. I don't know what
              to do.

                              VERNA
              It's all right, son. Stewart and
              I'll take the next plane to Los
              Angeles.

                              STEWART
              Verna, what's going on?

                                            (CONTINUED)

                              VERNA
                    Just get dressed and pack some
                    things for us.
                              (into phone)
                    Duane, what's the address where
                    your're at?

                              DUANE
                    The... the Marco Apartments. On
                    5th and Western Street.

                              VERNA
                    And that name you're using,
                    Richard what?

                              DUANE
                    Davis. But, Ma, I can't stay
                    here.

                              VERNA
                    Get hold of yourself, son. I'll
                    leave right away. But first...
                    now, Duane, listen carefully;
                    you can't let them find what
                    you've done... like the last
                    time. Know what I mean? This
                    time you must get rid of it.

                              DUANE
                    No! No, I can't.

                              VERNA
                    Listen to me, darling — while
                    it's still dark, you've got to
                    take it out in the woods
                    somewhere... and bury it.

                              DUANE
                    Bury it...

                              VERNA
                    That's right. Then come back to
                    your room and wait for us.

                              DUANE
                    I'll try... But hurry...

STAY with Duane. As he hangs up, he is alarmed by the
SOUND of a POLICE SIREN APPROACHING. He springs over
to the window, pulls the shade back slightly and peeks
out. The SIREN passes, SOUND DIMINISHING.

                                                    (CONTINUED)

5   CONTINUED: (2)   5

       Looking back into the room, it seems to be closing in
       on him. Confused, frightened, he turns his attention
       to the girl's body... and braces himself to do what
       must.be done... and we:

                                                    CUT TO:

6   EXT. JONES' OFFICE BUILDING - ESTABLISHING (STOCK) -   6
       DAY

7   INT. JONES' OFFICE - DAY   7

       BETTY stands on tiptoe on a three-step ladder return-
       ing books to the top shelf of the bookcase when she
       HEARS something behind her. She turns and is star-
       tled to see —

8   STEWART COMPTON   8

       standing just inside the doorway staring at her legs.

9   WIDER ANGLE   9

       Disconcerted, Betty quickly.steps down off the ladder.

                         BETTY
                 Oh! I... didn't hear you come
                 in.

                         STEWART
                 Ah... looking for the Barnaby
                 Jones that's listed in the phone
                 book as an investigator.

                         BETTY
                 I expect him back in a little
                 while. Can I help you?

                         STEWART
                     (calls)
                 Verna...!

10   ANOTHER ANGLE   10

       to SHOW Verna in the outer office, nosily browsing
       through the things on Betty's desk; letters, papers,
       etc. She turns, sees Betty looking her way, and
       breezes in:

                                                    (CONTINUED)

                              VERNA
                    Oh, there is someone here.
                              (extends hand)
                    I'm Verna Davis. My husband,
                    Stewart.

                              BETTY
                    Betty Jones. Barnaby's daughter-
                    in-law. What is it you want to
                    see him about?

                              VERNA
                    My son, Duane...
                              (produces
                              photo)
                    ... This bright lovely boy. He's
                    disappeared. Vanished.

Betty takes the picture, studies it.

11   INSERT OF PHOTO   11

It is a 3 X 5 of Duane wearing his high school graduation cap and gown.

                              VERNA (O.S.)
                    Richard's a good boy; never been
                    in trouble in his life.

12   RESUME SCENE   12

                              BETTY
                    Richard?... Didn't you call him
                    Duane a moment ago?

                              VERNA
                    Did I? Well, he goes by Richard
                    now; thinks it's more manly.
                    Only I just can't get used to
                    it.

Betty clips the photo to a pad and starts taking notes.

                              BETTY
                    Richard Davis... his height,
                    weight?

                              VERNA
                    Just under six feet tall. Brown
                    hair and eyes. About a hundred
                    seventy/seventy-five pounds.
                    And he just turned twenty-two.

                              127   (CONTINUED)

                        BETTY
              When was the last time you were in
              touch with Richard?

                        VERNA
              I talked to him on the phone
              last night about flying in
              from Denver. That's where we
              live...

                        BETTY
                   (incredulous)
              He's only been missing since...
              last night?!

                        VERNA
                   (nodding)
              And when we got here this
              morning, he'd already checked
              out of his room, bag and
              baggage. Didn't even leave
              a forwarding address.

                        BETTY
              Mrs. Davis — the thing is, Barnaby
              doesn't usually handle ordinary
              cases of missing persons...

                        VERNA
                   (distressed)
              He doesn't?...

When Verna has need for tears, they come:

                        VERNA
                   (continuing)
              Stewart... what am I going to
              do?

Stewart mutters something and shrugs. He isn't the
best straight man in the world.

                        BETTY
              I'm sure your son is just as
              anxious to reestablish contact
              as you. I wouldn't be surprised
              if he hasn't already tried calling
              you at home.

                        VERNA
              But there's nobody back in Denver
              to answer the phone.

                                        (CONTINUED)

                    STEWART
          It's for sure we don't have the
          money to be flying back and forth.

                    VERNA
          What's got me worried most is
          that Richard's a sick boy. It's
          dangerous for him to be on his
          own because he gets these...
          spells. I'm so afraid something
          terrible will happen unless we
          find him right away.

                    BETTY
                    (beat)
          All right... I'll see what I
          can do.

                    VERNA
                    (brightens)
          You will?... Oh, I knew it.
          Right off you struck me as a very
          human type of person.

                    BETTY
          Problem is, where to start? I
          imagine, if you knew of any
          friends he had in town you'd
          have already tried them.

                    VERNA
          Richard doesn't make friends
          easily.

                    BETTY
          What about a job — was he
          working?

                    VERNA
          He said something about having
          a job, only I didn't think to
          ask what it was.

                    STEWART
          Y'know... could be he got himself
          into some kind of carpentry work.

                    BETTY
          If he's in the carpenter's union,
          it would sure narrow it down some.

                                        (CONTINUED)

                              STEWART
               He's not. But being a carpenter
               myself, every now and then I'd
               scab him onto a job so's he
               could pick up a couple dollars.
               The boy wasn't good for much
               else.

                              VERNA
                        (takes umbrage)
               That's your trouble, Stewart.
               Always looking down your nose at
               him just because he's a step-son.

                              BETTY
               I'll start checking around...

       Taking the notes with her, Betty cues them to exit
       by crossing into —

13   INT. BETTY'S OUTER OFFICE   13

       Verna and Stewart follow.

                              BETTY
               ... If I turn up anything, where
               can I get in touch with you?

                              VERNA
               It's all been so hectic, I'm
               afraid we haven't had time to
               take a room yet.

                              BETTY
               Then call me later. Before six.

                              VERNA
               Thank you, Betty. And bless you.

14   ANOTHER ANGLE   14

       As Verna and Stewart turn for the door, it opens and
       BARNABY and J.R. sail in, quickly stepping aside to
       avoid a collision.

                              JONES
               Excuse me.

                              VERNA
               No harm done, darlin'.

                                             (CONTINUED)

Barnaby looks after her as she and Stewart exit, then he and J.R., busy men, continue into Barnaby's office.

> J.R.
> The insurance company send over the list of items stolen from Ruddock's warehouse yet, Betty?

15   INT. JONES' OFFICE   15

Betty, grabbing some papers from her desk, is following them in.

> BETTY
> The list for you...
>   (hands it to J.R.)
> And Mr. Ruddock's market value estimate of the items stolen.

Which she hands to Barnaby.

> JONES
> Those people who just left, what was that about?

> BETTY
> They wanted to hire you to find their son who's been missing since last night.

> J.R.
> Last night — ?!

> BETTY
> That's what I said. But she was so upset, I couldn't help but take pity on her.

> JONES
> You didn't say I would take the case, did you?

> BETTY
> Of course not. I said I would.

> J.R.
> Then who's going to type these reports? They have to be ready by this afternoon.

(CONTINUED)

> BETTY
> Don't panic, J.R. All I have to
> do for those people is make
> some phone calls...
> (crossing out)
> I'll get the work done.

16   INT. BETTY'S OFFICE   16

Entering, Betty closes Barnaby's door, sits at her
desk, frowns at the photo of Duane and the scant notes
she took from Verna, then picks up the phone, starts
to dial, and we:

CUT TO:

17   EXT. LUMBER YARD - DAY   17

ESTABLISHING, then NARROW ON the burly 35-year-old
foreman, WINCHELL, who is moving a load of lumber on
a forklift when he spots Duane hurrying towards the
office.

> WINCHELL
> Hey, Davis — !

Duane alters course and comes to the foreman, who
holds him with a frosty look as he pulls the lift to
a stop and gets off.

> WINCHELL
> (continuing)
> Look, goof-off, you've been
> working here only a month and
> you're already late five times!

Unshaven, his body crying for sleep, Duane keeps looking over his shoulder as if demons are after him.

> DUANE
> I'm sorry, Mr. Winchell.
> Something's come up, and —

> WINCHELL
> No more excuses or you're out
> on your can. Come on. I'm
> gonna need a hand unloading
> this stuff.

(CONTINUED)

                              DUANE
            I can't. I have to leave town
            right away. I've come for my
            pay.

                              WINCHELL
            You're quitting — ?!

                              DUANE
                    (nodding)
            I've got two weeks' pay coming.
            If I could have it now, I'd
            appreciate it.

Winchell is getting back on the forklift:

                              WINCHELL
            Right now, huh? Leaves me
            shorthanded and it's favors he
            wants yet. The accountant'll
            be here tomorrow around eleven.
            Cry in his beer; okay?!

                              DUANE
            But I have to go away. I need
            the money now!

                              WINCHELL
                Tough.

And he puts the lift in motion and drives away. Frus-
trated, angry, Duane thrusts his hand inside his
jacket, as if to reach for a gun... then stops, decides
that won't get him anywhere... then turns and starts
away...

                                           CUT TO:

18   EXT. BETTY'S APARTMENT - ESTABLISHING - NIGHT (STOCK)   18

19   INT. BETTY'S APARTMENT - NIGHT   19

Having changed into a comfortable lounging outfit,
Betty is unpacking a delicate ceramic figurine she'd
bought and is seeing how it looks on the coffee table
when the DOOR CHIME SOUNDS. Leaving it on the chain,
she opens the door and is astonished to see it's Verna
and Stewart.

                                           (CONTINUED)

                         VERNA
        It's us. Hope you don't mind
        us dropping over like this,
        Betty.

                         BETTY
        Ah... no, that's all right...

                         VERNA
                    (peers past her)
        My... what a lovely apartment.

                         BETTY
                    (removing chain)
        Oh, yes. Please, come in...
                    (as they do)
        If you don't mind my asking,
        how did you get my address?

                         VERNA
        Wasn't easy, considering how
        many Jones there are in the
        phone book. Lucky thing I was
        able to match one up with the
        bill from Carstairs Department
        Store I saw on your desk. This
        is for you...
                    (presents gift box)
        ... Chocolate covered cherries.
        Grandma always said: never
        visit empty handed.

                         BETTY
                    (accepting box)
        Thank you... I expected you to
        call the office.

                         VERNA
        I did. Didn't I, Stewart? But
        you'd already gone...
                    (then)
        I can see it in your face —
        nothing, huh?
                    (before Betty
                     can reply)
        Oh, I know something dreadful's
        happened to that boy.

                         STEWART
        Here now, Verna. Don't fret so.
        The lady's doing the best she
        can, I'm sure.
                         (MORE)

                                        (CONTINUED)

                                   STEWART (CONT'D)
                              (to Betty)
                    She's got to get off her feet
                    a while.

                                   BETTY
                    Of course... Please, sit down.

Stewart guides Verna onto the couch, then also sits.

                                   BETTY
                              (continuing)
                    Would you like some coffee...
                    tea?

                                   VERNA
                              (tapping heart)
                    No stimulants, the doctor said.
                              (laments)
                    That boy... That boy...

                                   BETTY
                    You haven't given me a chance...
                    but I did turn up one possible
                    lead.

                                   VERNA
                    You did?

                                   BETTY
                    One of the jobbers I talked to
                    who hire non-union carpenters,
                    said he can't remember the name,
                    but that a young man fitting
                    Richard's description left him
                    for a job in a lumberyard.

                                   VERNA
                    You hear that, Stewart?

Stewart, who during this has picked up the new ceramic
and is looking it over, responds with a desultory nod.
For reasons we will later understand, Duane's welfare
is not his major concern.

                                   VERNA
                              (continuing; to
                              Betty)
                    He say which lumberyard?

Stewart's handling of the ceramic is making Betty more
and more uncomfortable, cuing her to want them gone as
quickly as possible:

                                             (CONTINUED)

                                   135

                              BETTY
                    No. But I've been going through
                    all the ones listed in the phone
                    book.
                              (edging for door)
                    If that doesn't turn up anything,
                    I'll try something else.

                              VERNA
                    Like what?

                              BETTY
                    Let's cross that bridge when
                    we come to it. Meanwhile, it's
                    been a long day, and I guess
                    we're all a bit tired and anxious
                    to get some sleep.

                              VERNA
                    Oh, yes. It's getting late.

Verna stirs to get up, then suddenly clutches at the
pain in her chest.

20   ANOTHER ANGLE   20

       as Stewart, who has been through this before, grabs
       for Verna's purse.

                              STEWART
                    Easy, Verna. Take it easy...

                              BETTY
                    What is it?

                              VERNA
                    Nothing... it's nothing.

       Stewart has gotten a bottle of pills from the purse.

                              STEWART
                    Her heart — acts up every now and
                    then. Could we have some water?

       Betty goes to get a glass of water while Stewart
       presses one of the pills into Verna's hand.

                              BETTY
                    Maybe I better call a doctor...?

                                                     (CONTINUED)

                         VERNA
          No, don't do that, Betty. I'll
          be all right. All I need is to
          rest for a few hours.

                         BETTY
                    (getting water)
          Your hotel... is it far from here?

                         VERNA
                    (sarcastic)
          Go on, Stewart, tell Betty where
          our hotel is.

                         STEWART
          Well... all the ones we looked
          at are pretty expensive. Gotta
          watch our pennies, y'know.

                         BETTY
                    (hands Verna glass)
          You still don't have a place to
          stay?

                         VERNA
                    (takes pill)
          Don't you pay it any mind.
                    (stirring to
                     rise)
          We'll find something.

                         STEWART
                    (restraining her)
          Verna, you're gonna kill yourself.

                         VERNA
          If I do, Stewart, it's not going
          to be on this kind lady's floor.
          Now let go.

                         STEWART
          Betty, talk to her.

                         BETTY
          Well... you could rest here, I
          guess, but...

                         VERNA
                    (quickly)
          Now isn't that a neighborly
          thing to do.

                                        (CONTINUED)

                                    BETTY
                              (feeling trapped)
                    ... Only I'm not really set up
                    for house guests...

                                    VERNA
                    Oh, never you mind about that.
                    The couch'll suit me just fine.
                    And Stewart can make a place
                    for himself by pushing the
                    ottoman up to the chair.

                                    BETTY
                    Ah... sure... ah, if you think
                    you'll be comfortable?...

                                    VERNA
                    Like two birds in a robin's
                    nest.

Betty has opened the closet door and is getting out
some blankets and pillows. Stewart relieves her of
them:

                                   STEWART
                    Here... I'll take care of that.

                                    VERNA
                    Right. We'll be no trouble to
                    you, so you go on to bed and
                    pay us no mind.
                              (on Betty's
                               hesitation)
                    'I was a stranger, and ye took
                    me in...' Matthew, chapter
                    twenty-five. Bless you, Betty.

Betty nods, then, concerned for the figurine, transfers
it from the coffee table to a safer place...

                                    BETTY
                    Well... I hope you're feeling
                    better in the morning
                              (at bedroom door)
                    Good night.

21   INT. BEDROOM - NIGHT   21

Betty enters, closes the door. She stands there a
moment, then punctuates her dismay with a shrug as
she starts to undress... and we:

                                             CUT TO:

22   EXT. BETTY'S APARTMENT HOUSE - RE-ESTABLISHING - DAY   22
      (STOCK)

23   INT. BETTY'S BEDROOM - DAY   23

      The curtains are drawn apart, flooding sunlight on
      Betty, who stands there in her pajamas breathing in
      the morning air. Then she suddenly remembers — the
      house guests! She picks up a robe and slips into it
      on the way to the door.

24   INT. LIVING ROOM - DAY   24

      Entering, Betty finds no one there; the pillows and
      blankets put away, the ottoman back where it belongs.
      Even the figurine is back on the coffee table. Verna
      and Stewart are apparently gone. Following her morning
      routine, she goes to the front door and opens it expect-
      ing to find the morning paper on the threshold.

25   INSERT - THE THRESHOLD   25

      No morning paper there.

26   RESUME SCENE   26

      Puzzled, Betty closes the door and is about to return
      to the bedroom when she hears a NOISE from the kitchen.
      Now a touch apprehensive, she goes to investigate.

27   INT. KITCHEN - DAY   27

      Verna and Stewart, seated at the table enjoying a
      hearty breakfast, look up at Betty, startled to see
      them.

                          VERNA
                Morning, Betty. Didn't know
                what time you'd be getting up
                or Stewart would've made enough
                eggs for you too.
                     (elbowing him)
                Stewart!

      Stewart rises and is opening the refrigerator to get
      the eggs when Betty, who can't help smiling at find-
      ing herself a guest in her own home, stops him:

                                        (CONTINUED)

                            139

                              BETTY
               Never mind... Don't worry about
               me...
                    (to Verna)
               I see you're feeling much better.

                              VERNA
               Not really. I won't feel myself
               again until I see my son; till I
               know that boy is well and safe.

                              STEWART
               You're a little low on orange
               juice, but we saved you some.

                              BETTY
               It's all right. I usually have
               something at the office. Anybody
               see the morning paper?

                              VERNA
               The paper...?

                              BETTY
                    (off their blank
                    looks)
               Wasn't there a paper outside the
               front door?

                              STEWART
               Never opened the door.

                              BETTY
                    (shrugs)
               It doesn't matter...
                    (off watch)
               Look... as long as you're here,
               stay for a couple more hours so
               I'll know where you can be
               reached. By then I hope I'll
               have better news for you. Okay?...

                              VERNA
                    (nodding)
               Really, Betty... I don't know
               what we would've done without
               you.

Betty smiles, exits to her bedroom to get dressed.

28   ANOTHER ANGLE   28

Stewart waits until he hears Betty's bedroom DOOR CLOSE.

                              140   (CONTINUED)

28 CONTINUED: 28

Then he opens the cupboard and retrieves the newspaper
from the waste bucket. They speak low so as not to be
heard by Betty:

                    STEWART
          What's gonna happen when she
          sees this?

Verna takes the paper and studies the front page
thoughtfully.

29 INSERT - NEWSPAPER   29

The headline reads: GIRL MURDER VICTIM FOUND IN
TOPANGA CANYON. The sub-headline: POLICE ARTIST
SKETCH OF UNIDENTIFIED MAN SEEN FLEEING SCENE. The
accompanying composite drawing, facial scratch marks
included, closely resembles the photo of Duane that
Verna gave Betty.

30 RESUME SCENE   30

                    STEWART
          Well? What if she recognizes
          that this is Duane?

                    VERNA
               (turns hostile)
          You'd like that, wouldn't you — ?!

                    STEWART
          No — !
               (he instantly avers)
          No, I like that boy. You know
          that.

                    VERNA
          No you don't. But it doesn't
          matter long as you keep it in
          your mind that I'm not going to
          let them take my son back to
          that awful hospital...
               (looking towards
                Betty's bedroom
                door)
          And if anybody gets in my way...
          I'll kill 'em...!

A beat, then...

                                        FADE OUT.

                    END OF ACT ONE
                         141

FADE IN:

31   EXT. JONES' OFFICE BUILDING - RE-ESTABLISH - DAY   31
      (STOCK)

32   INT. JONES' OFFICE - DAY   32

      CLOSE ON front page of newspaper with composite draw-
      ing of Duane we previously saw in Betty's kitchen.
      WIDEN TO SCENE, REVEALING it is J.R. holding the paper
      open to an inside page. He finds what he's looking
      for, folds the paper so that the front page is no
      longer visible, and starts for Betty's door. Barnaby
      is SEEN busy at his desk.

33   INT. BETTY'S OFFICE - DAY   33

      Betty is typing furiously while waiting for a response
      from someone at the other end of the telephone which
      she has propped to her ear. As J.R. enters:

                         BETTY
                    Yes... Richard Davis... I'll
                    hold on.

                         J.R.
                      (from paper)
                    Ruddock's container ship, The
                    Ocean Traveller, left Long
                    Beach Harbor at 7:10 this
                    morning. Make sure that's in
                    the report. Okay?

      Betty has been taking it down.

                         BETTY
                    Got it.

      INTERCUT Barnaby:

                         JONES
                      (calls)
                    Betty... How's it coming? We
                    have to head back to Long
                    Beach before lunch.

                         BETTY
                      (calls back)
                    I'm almost finished, Barnaby...
                         (MORE)

                                              (CONTINUED)

142

                              BETTY (CONT'D)
                           (into phone)
                    He doesn't work there?... Thanks.

          She hangs up, checks off another lumber yard listing
          in the phone book, continues typing as:

                              JONES
                    Are you still on that missing
                    son business?

                              J.R.
                    Is she ever...
                           (teasing her)
                    ... Betty's so dedicated she even
                    had her clients overnight as
                    houseguests.

          Betty rises and steps into the doorway.

                              BETTY
                    Big mouth.

                              JONES
                    Overnight? Betty, you think maybe
                    you'd better fill us in on what
                    it's all about?

          Betty rises and steps into the doorway.

                              BETTY
                    There's really nothing much to
                    tell, Barnaby. After I got
                    home last night —

          The RING of the TELEPHONE interrupts.

34   ANOTHER ANGLE   34

          as Betty gestures at the interruption, closes the door,
          returns to her desk and answers the phone:

                              BETTY
                    Barnaby Jones Investigations.

35   INT. LUMBER YARD OFFICE - DAY   35

          Winchell is on the other end of the line:

                              WINCHELL
                    Yeah, this is the foreman at
                    Redwood Lumber.
                           (MORE)

                                                        (CONTINUED)
                                   143

                                        WINCHELL (CONT'D)
                         I got a note here that you called
                         yesterday. What can I do for you?

INTERCUT Betty.

                                        BETTY
                         It's in reference to a Richard
                         Davis. The clerk I spoke to
                         said the name sounded familiar,
                         but that —

                                        WINCHELL
                         What about Davis?

                                        BETTY
                         Then he does work there?

                                        WINCHELL
                         Not anymore. The little creep
                         quit on me yesterday.

                                        BETTY
                         Oh no...

                                        WINCHELL
                         What's this about? He in some
                         kind of trouble, I hope?

                                        BETTY
                         Nothing like that. His mother
                         is in from out of town and asked
                         me to look for him.

                                        WINCHELL
                         Yeah... Well, tell her to drop
                         by here in five or ten minutes.
                         Her baby boy is gonna show up
                         around then for his final check.

END INTERCUT. STAY with Betty.

                                        BETTY
                         He is — ?

There is a CLICK on the other end of the line as
Winchell abruptly hangs up. With a bright sense of
accomplishment, she starts to jot down the address
of the lumber yard, as we —

                                                              CUT TO:

                                     144

Stewart is washing the breakfast dishes while Verna
sits at the table frowning at her newly applied makeup
in a mirror.

> VERNA
> Look at that... Can't hardly
> blame Duane if he said his
> mother's getting to look like
> a dried prune.

Stewart stops what he's doing and looks at her with
eyes that see the woman she was when he first married
her:

> STEWART
> Don't go putting yourself down,
> Verna. To me... you're still
> the most beautiful woman I've
> ever known...

As much as Verna can be touched, she is:

> VERNA
> You're a good man, Stewart.
> Duane's father, Billy... he
> was headstrong, didn't listen...
> (warmed by memory)
> But he sure knew how to make me
> jealous; handsome devil. Still...
> keeping a steady job, like you;
> supporting a home... That's
> important, too...

Even in bestowing a compliment she manages to stab him
with an odious comparison, albeit unintentionally. The
PHONE RINGS. Verna grabs it:

> VERNA
> (continuing)
> Hello...

INTERCUT Betty.

> BETTY
> Verna, Betty. I have good news...

> VERNA
> You found him!

> BETTY
> I think so, but you've got to
> get there fast, before he gets
> away again.

                                        (CONTINUED)

145

                         VERNA
          Where?...
                  (to Stewart)
          My bag — quick.

He hands it to her. She gets out pen and pad, writes:

                         BETTY
          Redwood Lumber Yard. Tell the
          taxi driver it's on Glendon
          Street and Wallace Avenue in
          East Los Angeles.

                         VERNA
          Won't need a taxi. We rented
          a car yesterday, so just tell
          me how to get there.

                         BETTY
          All right. Get on the downtown
          freeway to the Wallace off ramp.
          Then stay on Wallace going east
          until you get to Glendon. That's
          it.

                         VERNA
                  (having difficulty)
          Ah... Wallace off ramp, huh?
          Then to Glendon?...

                         BETTY
          East to Glendon. Look... there
          isn't much time. I'm closer, so
          I better drive over there and
          make sure you don't miss Richard;
          in case you have any trouble finding
          the place.

                         VERNA
          We're on our way.

END INTERCUT. STAY with Betty.

After hanging up, Betty turns back to the typewriter
and quickly finishes the last line of the report,
then she rips it out of the machine, picks up the
other pages of the report and hurries into —

37   INT. BARNABY'S OFFICE   37

where she crosses to place the report on his desk.

                                        (CONTINUED)

                         BETTY
              There's the report, Barnaby.

                         JONES
              Okay, Let's go.

    ... he says, rising, putting the report in an envelope.

                         BETTY
              I've got to wrap up that little
              missing persons case of mine,
              Barnaby. So I'll have to meet
              you in Long Beach.

                         JONES
              Found your man that fast, huh?
              Congratulations.

    She is on the fly, exiting:

                         J.R.
                    (calling after)
              Yeah... they should all be that
              easy.

                         BETTY
              Nothing, fellas. Nothing at all...

    And she's gone.

                                        CUT TO:

38   EXT. LUMBER YARD OFFICE - DAY   38

    Outside the office, standing by a lumber-loaded pickup
    truck, a driver signs the receipt and hands it over to
    Winchell.

                         WINCHELL
              And don't make delivering this
              load your life's work. Okay?!

    Turning away, Winchell spots Duane coming. He wears
    a bandage to cover the scratch marks. Winchell frowns
    and continues into the office; Duane hurrying after...

39   INT. LUMBER YARD OFFICE - DAY   39

    Winchell steps over to his desk and is in the process
    of filing the receipt when Duane enters.

                                        (CONTINUED)

                            DUANE
                    Hello, Mr. Winchell. My paycheck
                    ready?

                            WINCHELL
                        (nodding)
                    Be with you in a minute.

Letting Duane cool his heels, Winchell takes his time
with the receipt.

40   ON DUANE   40

fidgeting, glancing nervously out the window...

41   WINCHELL   41

finishes with the receipt and is picking up a batch of
newly issued checks that are lying on top of the morning newspaper. The item catches his eye...

42   INSERT - THE MORNING NEWSPAPER   42

and the composite drawing of the girl-killer suspect.

43   RESUME SCENE   43

as Duane, turning from the window, reacts to the funny
way Winchell is studying him.

                            DUANE
                    What's the matter...?

                            WINCHELL
                        (sneaks another glance
                         at paper)
                    Nothing... Just looking for the
                    check...
                        (then)
                    You really must've gotten into
                    a donnybrook the other night,
                    getting your face scratched up
                    like that.

Duane's hand shoots up to the bandage on his face.

                            DUANE
                    How do you know I got scratched?

                                                          (CONTINUED)

> WINCHELL
> Saw it when you came by
> yesterday.
>   (stalling)
> Look... ah... seems they didn't
> send the check over in this batch.

> DUANE
> What are you trying to pull?!

> WINCHELL
> No problem. I'll just call the
> main office and have 'em send it
> right over.

So saying, he exits into a side office to make the
call.

44   ANOTHER ANGLE   44

By now, Duane is highly suspicious of the foreman.
Drifting over to the desk, he looks at the phone
lying on it and wonders why Winchell had to use one
in the side office. Then he spots the newspaper with
the composite drawing of himself. Drawing a gun, **Duane**
moves to the side office door, bending close to listen.

45   INT. LUMBER YARD SIDE OFFICE - DAY   45

Winchell is on the phone, dialing the last digit.

> WINCHELL
> Hello. Yeah, Sergeant — I want
> to talk to somebody about the
> picture of that guy in today's
> paper...

Just then the door bangs open. He freezes at the
sight of Duane menacing him with the gun.

> DUANE
> Hang up! Right now — !

> WINCHELL
>   (doing so)
> Take it easy with that
> thing...

> DUANE
> Get back in here!

149

46   EXT. LUMBER YARD OFFICE - DAY   46

Betty drives in, parks the Pinto near the office, gets
out...

47   INT. LUMBER YARD OFFICE - DAY   47

His back to the front door, Duane keeps a distance
between himself and Winchell, who is coming out of
the side office with his hands up.

                    WINCHELL
          Look, kid... the check is here.
          I'll get it for you...

                    DUANE
          Won't be able to cash it now.
          I want my money from the box
          you keep in the drawer.

                    WINCHELL
          Sure...

He is moving to the desk, when —

48   BETTY   48

sails in.

                    BETTY
          Hi there. Is Richard Da—

The question gets caught in her throat as Duane whirls
about, brandishing the gun.

                    DUANE
          Shut up and don't make a sound!
                    (gestures)
          Get over there!

Betty stares in shock.

                    WINCHELL
          Better do as he says, ma'am.
                    (indicates paper)
          He's the killer the police are
          looking for.

Betty looks over at the composite drawing.

                    DUANE
          Go on, get over there — !

49   WINCHELL   49

takes advantage of the distraction and lunges at Duane,
grabbing hold of his wrist.

50   ANOTHER ANGLE   50

Winchell, more powerful than Duane, wrenches him
around and bats his wrist against the wall, knocking
the gun from Duane's hand.

51   BETTY   51

in the corner, blocked from the exit by the grappling
men, makes a move to retrieve the gun that falls on
the floor. As she does —

52   WINCHELL   52

pushes Duane away from him, goes for the gun, picks it
up before Betty can reach it and turns it on Duane,
just as —

53   DUANE   53

grabs a piece of lumber, raises it.

54   WINCHELL   54

squeezes off a SHOT.

55   DUANE   55

reacts to being shot, but still manages to wield the
piece of lumber. It flashes PAST CAMERA...

56   WIDER ANGLE   56

Winchell reacts to being hit, sprawls on the floor un-
conscious. Betty is edging for the door when Duane,
clutching the wound in his side, picks up the gun and
turns it on her.

                        DUANE
            Stop!

She does. He goes to the window, looks out.

                        151

57   POV THROUGH WINDOW   57

Betty's car in the f.g. In the distance, one of the
yard workers is SEEN looking this way, apparently in
reaction to having heard the shot.

58   RESUME SCENE   58

as Duane goes to the door, opens it.

                         DUANE
               That your car?
                    (on Betty's nod)
               All right. You're going to
               drive us out of here.

                         BETTY
               You... don't look like you're
               in any shape to travel.

                         DUANE
               Go on — !

With some apprehension, she obeys...

59   EXT. INTERSECTION NEAR LUMBER YARD - DAY   59

The Ford driven by Stewart, with Verna in the passenger
seat, stops at the intersection for cross traffic.

                         STEWART
               There it is.

He is about to drive on when Verna spots them:

                         VERNA
               Wait! It's Duane...

60   THEIR POV - THE LUMBER YARD   60

They see Duane, holding a gun on Betty, cross to her
Pinto and get in. And much farther beyond, three yard
workers approaching to investigate...

61   RESUME ON VERNA AND STEWART   61

                         STEWART
               He looks like he's been hurt...

Verna watches, keeping her cool...

62   THE APPROACHING YARD WORKERS   62

      SHOOTING PAST them, the Pinto is SEEN wheeling out of
      the yard...

63   VERNA AND STEWART IN THE FORD   63

                           VERNA
          Follow them...

      Stewart puts the car in motion, and follows after the
      speeding Pinto...

                                 CUT TO:

64   INT. BETTY'S CAR - MOVING - DAY   64

      Betty keeps one eye on the road and one on Duane —
      who is quickly slipping from consciousness... when
      his head rolls to one side, Betty decides to...

65   EXT. DESERTED INDUSTRIAL AREA - DAY   65

      Betty's car comes to a stop.

66   INT. BETTY'S CAR   66

      CLOSE ON Duane. He is slumped back, semi-conscious,
      muttering incoherently, the gun clutched in his hand.

67   REVERSE ANGLE   67

      Betty considers taking the gun from him, then resists
      the impulse, afraid she might rouse him. Instead, she
      eases open the door...

68   EXT. BETTY'S CAR - WIDER ANGLE   68

      Betty is carefully getting out of the car as the Ford
      races in, brakes to a stop. Verna and Stewart get out
      and rush over. Betty turns, surprised:

                         BETTY
          How did you...?

                         VERNA
              (ignoring Betty)
        Duane... Duane...

                           (CONTINUED)

Stewart opens the passenger door and Verna, giving vent
to her anguish, presses in to her son's side.

> VERNA
> (continuing)
> Oh, honey... what have they done
> to you?...
> (on Duane's moan)
> It's all right, baby. Mother's
> here. Everything's all right now.

> STEWART
> He's bleeding bad.

> BETTY
> I'm going to call an ambulance.

As she starts for the corner public phone booth:

> VERNA
> (stops her with)
> No ambulance! He'll be all
> right, we'll take care of him.

> BETTY
> Verna — he's been shot. He
> could die...

> VERNA
> He's not going to be locked up
> again, you hear — ?!
> (gets Duane's gun;
> levels it on Betty)
> Never! They're never going to
> take him from me again — !

69   ON BETTY   69

staring at the woman with disbelief... then...

> FADE OUT.

END OF ACT TWO

FADE IN:

70   EXT. SAME INDUSTRIAL AREA STREET - DAY   70

Not so deserted now. LIEUTENANT BIDDLE is among the
police going over Betty's Pinto. He looks up, sees
Barnaby and J.R. speed in... and steps over to greet
them.

                    BIDDLE
          Barnaby... J.R... I'm glad your
          exchange was able to locate you...

With grave faces that match Biddle's, Barnaby and
J.R. acknowledge with a nod, never taking their eyes
off the Pinto as they circle around it, studying it...

                    BIDDLE
                 (continuing)
          ... When I heard communications
          broadcast the DMV on it, I
          dropped everything and came
          right over.

                    JONES
          I take it there are no witnesses.

                    BIDDLE
                 (shaking head)
          A black and white spotted it,
          parked in the red, stopped to have
          a look, saw all that blood on the
          front seat and called it in.

                    J.R.
                 (clutching at straw)
          Then there's no way of knowing
          for sure Betty was in the car
          when whatever happened happened.

                    BIDDLE
          If it was stolen, she would've
          reported it by now, wouldn't she?

                    J.R.
          Yeah... I guess...

                    JONES
          Doesn't appear to be any blood
          on the driver's side.

                              (CONTINUED)

155

                         BIDDLE
             Meaning the driver was injured in
             some way after moving over to
             the passenger side... or there
             was more than one person in the
             car.

J.R. takes interest in the trail of blood that leads
away from the car and follows it... Meanwhile, Barnaby has taken a plastic evidence bag from his pocket
and scrapes some of the blood from the seat into it.

                         JONES
             You mind?

                         BIDDLE
             Of course not... Assuming the
             car wasn't stolen... any idea
             what Betty was doing that would
             bring her to this out-of-the-way
             part of town?

                         JONES
                   (shakes head)
             When she left the office, she
             was on her way to help some
             people who were trying to
             contact their son.

                         J.R. (O.S.)
             Barnaby...

71   ANOTHER ANGLE   71

J.R. is standing where the Ford stopped earlier,
scrutinizing the ground. As Barnaby and Biddle
step over:

                         J.R.
             Look at this. The blood trails
             from Betty's car to here... then
             stops.

                         JONES
             Mmmmmm... like whoever was hurt
             got into another car.

                         BIDDLE
             That's how we've got it figured...
                   (MORE)

                                        (CONTINUED)

                         BIDDLE (CONT'D)
                    (then)
               These people Betty was helping,
               better give me their names.

                         J.R.
               Don't know their names. We've
               been busy on another case and
               never really got into it with
               Betty.

                         JONES
               But she probably made notes.
               We'll be in touch.

As he and J.R. get back in the car and drive away, we:

                                        CUT TO:

72   EXT. EMERGENCY HOSPITAL - DAY   72

      It's a small neighborhood hospital. PAN OFF building
      and sign identifying it TO the Ford making a turn off
      the street into the parking area...

73   INT. FORD - DAY   73

      Betty is in the passenger seat beside Stewart.
      Verna, busy in the back trying to staunch Duane's
      bleeding with bandages (and medical supplies) they
      picked up earlier, is startled by them coming to a
      stop and brandishes the gun.

                         VERNA
               What are we stopping for...?

                         STEWART
               Verna... I don't think those
               bandages and stuff we got at the
               drugstore's gonna be enough...

      By now Verna, looking out, realizes where they are
      and is furious:

                         VERNA
               Damn you, Stewart! Didn't I
               tell you hospitals've got to
               report gunshot wounds? Now
               drive out of here — !

                                        (CONTINUED)

Betty, restraining Stewart's hand on the ignition
key, voices her own anger:

> BETTY
> Don't you do it!
> (to Verna)
> Are you crazy?! That boy needs
> a doctor.

> VERNA
> (falters)
> I know how to take care of him.
> He'll be all right.

> BETTY
> No, he won't! He's going to
> bleed to death — right in
> your arms!!

Verna considers... relents:

> VERNA
> I'll look things over first...
> (giving gun to
> Stewart)
> If she tries anything... you
> know what to do...

She gets out of the car and heads for the hospital
side door.

74   INT. HOSPITAL LOBBY - DAY   74

A few patients and relatives on the lower part of
the economic scale are in evidence. DAVID OXFORD,
34, lean, bespectacled black doctor, is off to the
side talking with one of the patients about to de-
part. Verna enters, is looking around as she
crosses to the desk. Fixing her attention on the
doctor, an idea forms in her mind as MISS ROSS, 28,
the duty nurse, steps in from a back room.

> MISS ROSS
> Can I help you?

> VERNA
> Indeed, Miss, I hope you can.
> You see, I am in great need of
> a doctor.

(CONTINUED)

                              MISS ROSS
                    Is it an emergency?

                              VERNA
                    Not really. Thing is, I'm
                    looking for a family doctor.
                    You know, one that has his own
                    private offices where he treats
                    his patients.

                              MISS ROSS
                    I'm afraid it's against hospital
                    policy to make such
                    recommendations. But if you
                    call the Medical Association —

                              VERNA
                         (overriding; indicating
                          Oxford)
                    Now what about that doctor there?
                    He doesn't just work here all the
                    time, does he?

                              MISS ROSS
                    Doctor Oxford? Oh, no. He has
                    his own practice. Works here
                    on weekends. Would you like to
                    talk to him?

                              VERNA
                    That's all right. I'll wait
                    till he's finished.

Miss Ross nods, returns to the back room.

75   ANOTHER ANGLE   75

What Verna is really waiting for is for Miss Ross to
be gone. Once she is, she moves quickly over and
interrupts:

                              VERNA
                    Doctor. Please, it's an
                    emergency.

                              OXFORD
                         (to patient)
                    Just be a minute.
                         (stepping over to
                          Verna)
                    What is it, ma'am?

                                              (CONTINUED)

                         VERNA
              Oh, please, Doctor, it's my son.
              He's out in the car, he's been
              hurt real bad.

                         OXFORD
              I'll have some orderlies bring
              out a gurney.

                         VERNA
              No, no! He shouldn't be moved
              until you see him first. Please,
              hurry. He may be dying — !

                         OXFORD
              All right. Let's have a look.

He follows Verna out.

76   EXT. PARKING LOT   76

Verna hurriedly leads Oxford to the car and opens the
rear door.

                         VERNA
              In here...

77   INT. CAR   77

Oxford gets in, reacts to Duane slumped in the seat
and takes his pulse.

                         OXFORD
              How did this happen?

Stewart is holding the gun low behind the front seat.
Verna reaches over and takes it from him as she gets
in the rear also and levels it on Oxford:

                         VERNA
              I'll tell you all about it on
              the way to your private offices,
              Doctor.

                         OXFORD
              Hey... what's going on — ?

                         BETTY
              You _are_ crazy!

                                        (CONTINUED)

>   VERNA
>   Stewart, what are you waiting
>   for?! Let's go!

78   OVERVIEW   78

as Stewart puts the Ford in motion and they barrel out
of the parking lot...

                                                   CUT TO:

79   INT. BETTY'S OFFICE - DAY   79

The front DOOR LOCK CLICKS open and in stride Barnaby
and J.R. Barnaby moves swiftly behind Betty's desk,
sits and begins leafing through her notebook. J.R.
is looking over his shoulder.

>   J.R.
>   There it is: Richard Davis...

>   JONES
>   Verna and Stewart Davis. Denver,
>   Colorado... a description...

>   J.R.
>   Everything except where Betty
>   was headed...

Jones is reaching for the phone book in which Betty
placed a book mark.

>   JONES
>   She was checking off numbers
>   out this...
>   (opening at
>   book mark)
>   Here we are — Lumber Yards.
>   The last one she checked off is...
>   (tracing down)
>   ... Redwood...

80   FAVORING J.R.   80

As Barnaby picks up the phone and dials the number,
J.R. pulls off the 3x5 graduation photo of Duane
clipped to the notebook page. He studies it closely,
something about it striking him as being familiar.

                                                   (CONTINUED)

> JONES
> (into phone)
> Hello... This is Barnaby Jones
> Investigations. I'm checking
> on a call made to you about two
> hours ago — from Betty Jones...
> (listens)
> Yes... she was making inquiries
> about a young man named Richard
> Davis...

During this: J.R. takes another hard look at Duane's
photo, then, remembering something, steps into —

81   INT. BARNABY'S OFFICE - DAY   81

... and looks around, spots the newspaper where he
had set it down earlier. During this:

> JONES (O.S.)
> ... There was a shooting? What
> happened? Who got shot?

J.R. reacts to what Barnaby is saying as he folds the
paper back to the front page. He compares the composite drawing with the graduation photo, then hurries
back to —

82   INT. BETTY'S OFFICE   82

where Barnaby is finishing the call:

> JONES
> Thank you very much.
> (hanging up)
> Someone there recognized a worker
> named Richard Davis and a woman
> get into a car matching Betty's
> ... and drive away.

> J.R.
> What was that about a shooting?

> JONES
> They're not clear on it. The
> foreman, a man named Winchell,
> was the only other person
> involved and he's still
> unconscious from a blow on
> the head.

(CONTINUED)

                              J.R.
                    Look at this...

J.R. first shows the graduation photo, then the composite drawing in the newspaper. Barnaby absorbs it
gravely.

                              J.R.
                          (continuing)
                    If that's the same Richard
                    Davis that Betty got into
                    the car with...

Enough said.

                            JONES
                    Get it over to Lieutenant
                    Biddle and fill him in.

                              J.R.
                    Right.

After J.R. goes, NARROW on a very worried Barnaby...

                                              CUT TO:

83   EXT. DOCTOR'S OFFICE - DAY   83

One of those converted bungalow-type houses in a
semiresidential street. The Ford is parked in the
driveway. With Verna bringing up the rear and Oxford
unlocking and opening the front door, Stewart and Betty
are helping Duane into the building...

                            VERNA
                    Careful with him... careful...

84   INT. WAITING ROOM - DAY   84

When all are in, Verna closes the door, locking it.

                            OXFORD
                    Let's get him into the examining
                    room. This way...

Oxford moves ahead to open the examining room door.
Verna is looking the place over.

                            VERNA
                    Anybody else here?

                                              (CONTINUED)

>   OXFORD
> It's Saturday. Everybody's off
> for the weekend.

85   INT. EXAMINING ROOM - DAY   85

>   OXFORD
> On the table... easy...

He helps Betty and Stewart place Duane on the table.

>   DUANE
>   (semiconscious)
> Mother...

>   VERNA
> Mother's right here, darling
> boy... You're going to be all
> right...

She wipes his forehead with a cloth. During the following, Oxford, with professional dispatch, is washing his
hands, then gets various medical aids from the cabinets.

>   BETTY
> Verna... he's lost so much blood.
> He needs to be in a hospital.

>   VERNA
> Get out!
>   (to Stewart,
>   handing him
>   the gun)
> Stay with her out there.

Using a pair of long surgical scissors, she begins
cutting away the clothes from Duane's wound.

>   BETTY
> Doctor... talk to her! Make
> her understand!

>   VERNA
> Out!

Stewart gestures with the gun. Betty exits, he follows.

86   ANOTHER ANGLE   86

Washed, instruments ready, Oxford has a stethoscope
to Duane's chest while at the same time is taking a
close look at the wound.

(CONTINUED)

                          OXFORD
               That lady's right. If I have
               to replace blood... or need
               life-support equipment... this
               sure isn't the place to be...

                          VERNA
                       (head in the
                         sand)
               I've had some nursing experience.
               I'll help.

                          OXFORD
                       (shrugs)
               Okay — scrub up. We'll have
               to go in for the bullet right
               away.

                          VERNA
               Just remember: if you're
               thinking of botching this up
               in order to make me take him
               to a hospital, I'll know...
               and I'll kill you.

                                          CUT TO:

87   INT. WAITING ROOM - DAY   87

      Betty sits on the couch, Stewart, gun hanging at his
      side, paces nervously.

                          BETTY
                       (beat)
               You... must love her very much...

      Stewart glances at Betty, but does not reply. He is
      a very troubled man.

                          BETTY
                       (continuing)
               You must, to do what you're
               doing for her...

                          STEWART
                       (with difficulty)
               Verna... Verna's really a good
               woman. You have to understand
               that.

                                          (CONTINUED)

> BETTY
> Please, let me call someone...
> if you love her, help me save
> her from killing her own son.
> There's still time...

Stewart is struggling with his emotions when they are
suddenly jolted by the SOUND of Duane CRYING OUT in
pain. Stewart jerks his head in that direction. As
he goes to the doorway to look in —

88   BETTY   88

rises from the couch and starts for a rear door.

89   OMITTED   89

90   INT. EXAMINING ROOM   90

Verna looks up and sees Betty dashing past the door,
heading for the rear door.

> VERNA
> Don't let her get away!

And a moment later, Stewart, gun in hand, rushes out
in pursuit. At this, realizing she is weaponless,
Verna brandishes the long surgical scissors and stands
ready to defend the door against any thought by Doctor
Oxford of escape. He, probing Duane's wound for the
bullet, regards her calmly:

> OXFORD
> Don't worry... I'm not going
> anywhere...

91   EXT. BACK YARD - DAY   91

Stewart comes rushing out, looks around. Betty is
gone. The alley leading off from the back yard seems
to be the only way she could have gone and he enters it.

92   EXT. ALLEY - DAY   92

Gun at the ready, coming on the run, Stewart looks
this way and that for Betty.

93   ANOTHER ANGLE   93

Farther into the alley, Stewart finds the way ob-
structed by a high brick wall; the alley is dead-
ended. If Betty came this way, then she must be
hiding somewhere. He searches, looking behind some
rubbish cans, behind the corner of a building, then
moves to some piled boxes...

94   ANOTHER ANGLE   94

As he pushes away the boxes, Betty is revealed crouch-
ing there. There is something pathetic, yet quite
deadly in his tone of voice:

                    STEWART
          If this is the way Verna wants
          it... then this is the way it's
          gonna be... let's go!

As Betty rises and starts back with Stewart following,
we:

                                        FADE OUT.

                    END OF ACT THREE

ACT FOUR

FADE IN:

95   EXT. JONES' OFFICE BUILDING - RE-ESTABLISH - DAY   95
(STOCK)

A TELEPHONE IS RINGING.

96   INT. JONES' LAB - DAY   96

The PHONE CONTINUES TO RING while Barnaby studies a
slide in the microscope. He looks up, grim, perturbed,
then reaches for the phone:

                    JONES
          Hello...

97   INT. LIEUTENANT BIDDLE'S OFFICE - DAY   97

Biddle listens attentively to J.R., who is on the other
end of the line to Barnaby, a document in J.R.'s hand.

                    J.R.
          Barnaby — a flyer out of Denver
          identifies Richard Davis as Duane
          Pierson, an escaped fugitive...

INTERCUT Barnaby as needed:

                    JONES
          Pierson?

                    J.R.
          Right — father dead, mother
          married again to a carpenter
          named Stewart Compton. Davis
          is just an alias they were all
          using.

                    JONES
          Then she must've known the
          trouble her son was in all
          the time...

                    J.R.
          It gets heavier: about eight
          months ago, his mother was given
          a suspended sentence for trying
          to help Duane escape from a
          Colorado hospital for the
          criminally insane.
                    (MORE)

                                        (CONTINUED)

168

                              J.R. (CONT'D)
                    The girl in the morning papers
                    isn't the first one he's killed...

Biddle picks up another phone, punching in to make it
a three-way conversation:

                              BIDDLE
                    Barnaby, every hospital in the
                    county's been alerted to report
                    all gunshot wounds directly to
                    me — and to be on the lookout
                    for anyone matching Duane or
                    Betty's description... We'll
                    find her.

                              JONES
                    Better be fast, John. I just
                    checked the blood from the car.
                    It's type-B. Same as Betty's.

                              J.R.
                    Don't throw in the towel, Barnaby.
                    Duane's blood is also type-B.

                              BIDDLE
                    We got it from Pierson's Denver
                    medical record.

                              JONES
                    ...A fifty/fifty chance on which
                    one's been hurt, I guess, is
                    better than nothing...

Barnaby hangs up, his anguish unabated. Then a thought
occurs to him. He gets up and quickly moves into...

98   INT. BARNABY'S OFFICE   98

Going to his desk, Barnaby searches a drawer, finds a
street map of the city, spreads it open and begins to
study it intently...

                                                      CUT TO:

99   INT. DOCTOR'S EXAMINING ROOM - DAY   99

CLOSE ON Duane. All is still except for his labored
breathing.

                                                (CONTINUED)

169

His face is flushed, sweaty. As ANGLE WIDENS, we SEE
Verna hovering close, her lips moving in silent prayer.
The silence is broken by the RING of the TELEPHONE.

100   THE SCENE   100

Oxford, who is adjusting the tube draining solution into Duane's nose, makes an involuntary move to answer
the PHONE.

                        VERNA
             I told you the last time: let it
             ring!

He does, turns back to finish the adjustment.

                        OXFORD
             He's not going to make it,
             unless we get him to a hospital.
             Now!

As if trying to heal Duane by osmosis, Verna stares at
her son, ignoring Oxford. Stewart, standing in the
doorway, shakes his head, then looks out at —

101   BETTY IN THE WAITING ROOM   101

Seated, her hands taped behind her, Betty becomes
suddenly very still on Stewart's looking her way.

                        OXFORD (O.S.)
                     (to Stewart)
             Mister... you've got to make your
             wife listen to reason...

When Stewart turns his look from Betty back at Oxford
in the examining room, Betty continues what she has
been doing — trying to cut through the tape that binds
her wrists by working it up and down against the edge
of a chrome side table.

102   RESUME IN EXAMINING ROOM   102

Getting no response from Stewart, either, anger rises
out of the doctor's frustration.

                        OXFORD
             Don't you people understand?!
                     (MORE)

                                              (CONTINUED)

                              OXFORD (CONT'D)
                    Sure, I got the bullet out, but
                    he's still burning up with fever
                    because I haven't been able to
                    stop the bleeding.

The TELEPHONE STOPS RINGING.

                              VERNA
                    I have eyes. The bleeding's
                    stopped. I can see that.

                              OXFORD
                    Not inside. He's hemorrhaging
                    internally!

                              VERNA
                         (a stone wall)
                    On my boy's life: if you let him
                    die, I'll kill you.

Oxford pleads with Stewart with a look.

                              STEWART
                         (hesitates)
                    Verna...

                              VERNA
                    No — ! They're not going to lock
                    him up in that place like an animal
                    for the rest of his life. We're
                    talking about my son!

Just then, Duane suddenly convulses, has difficulty
breathing.

                              VERNA
                         (continuing)
                    Oh my God...

Oxford quickly grabs the mouthpiece of a portable re-
suscitator, jams it over Duane's mouth and turns on
the oxygen. Verna's eyes widen with growing apprehension...

103   INT. WAITING ROOM   103

CLOSE ON Betty's hands as she continues to work the
tape against the table edge.

                                             (CONTINUED)

171

WIDENING TO SCENE, she abruptly stops the action as
Stewart, with it all weighing heavily on his mind,
turns from the grim scene in the examining room and
steps into the waiting room.

> VERNA (O.S.)
> Help him, Doctor. Don't let him
> die...

> BETTY
> (pleads with Stewart)
> There's the phone. Make the call.
> There still may be time.

Stewart studies Betty with a strange look, then stares
off, as if coming to terms with the dilemma that
plagues him:

> STEWART
> I'd have Verna all to myself...

> BETTY
> What...?

> STEWART
> If the boy does die... she'd have
> only me to turn to... I'd have her
> all to myself...

She stares at him in disbelief.

> VERNA (O.S.)
> Oh, please, Doctor... My poor
> baby... Help him...

Stewart drifts back towards —

104   THE EXAMINING ROOM   104

where he stops in the doorway and sees Oxford pounding
on Duane's chest in an effort to revive him...

> VERNA
> You're hurting him — !

She cries irrationally, tugging at Oxford. He moves
her back, then pounds again.

105   INT. WAITING ROOM   105

as Stewart looks back at Betty...

                                                    CUT TO:

J.R. is returning from police headquarters, finds
Barnaby on the phone:

> JONES
> ... That's right. The type of
> wound I have in mind would've
> been made by a gunshot, but it
> might not necessarily have been
> identified as such...
>   (listens)
> ... Thank you.

He hangs up.

> J.R.
> What's that all about?

Barnaby is getting another number off a list, and dials
while he explains:

> JONES
> Considering the amount of blood
> in Betty's car, I figure whoever
> was wounded couldn't have gotten
> too far without some kind of
> medical attention...

> J.R.
> But I heard Lieutenant Biddle
> tell you he's alerted all the
> hospitals.

> JONES
> In the county...
>   (indicates on map)
> ... I'm concentrating on hospitals
> in the immediate vicinity of where
> the car was found.

> J.R.
> They'd report a wound soon as
> any of the rest.

> JONES
> Maybe, maybe not — depending
> on the circumstances.

J.R. is sympathetic with Barnaby's need to be doing
something, even if it does seem hopeless.

(CONTINUED)

                              J.R.
                    Yeah... sure, Barnaby. I might
                    as well try some of 'em, too,
                    huh?...

          He selects the next number on the list and moves to
          another phone as Barnaby's call is answered:

                              JONES
                          (into phone)
                    Hello... I'm making inquiries
                    about a gunshot victim you may
                    have treated today...

107   INT. EMERGENCY HOSPITAL - DAY   107

          Miss Ross is at the lobby desk on the phone with
          Barnaby. INTERCUT as necessary.

                              MISS ROSS
                    A gunshot wound today?

                              JONES
                    Yes. Or one that could've been
                    made by a bullet, but —

                              MISS ROSS
                          (overriding)
                    Sir... sir, before you go on...
                    As it happens, Doctor Oxford,
                    our duty doctor up and disappeared
                    earlier this afternoon, so all
                    serious injuries are being routed
                    straight on to other hospitals.

                              JONES
                    Your doctor... disappeared?
                    What's that about?

          J.R. picks up on this, stops dialing his number.

                              MISS ROSS
                    It's a mystery to us. The last
                    anyone saw of him was when he
                    stepped outside with some woman.

                              JONES
                    A woman — do you know who she is?

                              MISS ROSS
                    No.
                          (MORE)

                                                      (CONTINUED)

                    MISS ROSS (CONT'D)
          Just some woman who wanted to know
          if he had offices away from the
          hospital where he treated patients.

                    JONES
          Have you tried him there?

                    MISS ROSS
          Yes. But nobody answers the phone.

                    JONES
          May I have that address, please.

END INTERCUT — STAY with Barnaby.

                    JONES
                (continuing; jots
                 it down)
          Thank you, ma'am.
                (to J.R.)
          Let's go.

And as they do, we...

                                        CUT TO:

108   INT. WAITING ROOM - DAY   108

Betty, still trying to cut the tape that binds her
wrists, stops as Oxford comes in from the examining
room, followed by Stewart. The doctor's wrists are
now also bound behind him with tape.

                    STEWART
          Better sit down...

Oxford obeys. She can read it on their faces:

                    BETTY
          He's dead...?
                (on Oxford's nod; at
                 Stewart)
          They're going to call it
          manslaughter. Kidnapping and
          manslaughter, because she kept
          him from receiving proper
          medical attention.

                    OXFORD
          When they put you two away, I
          hope they throw away the key.

                                        (CONTINUED)

> STEWART
> (losing his nerve)
> No! Verna will explain. The
> judge'll understand.

> BETTY
> All right, maybe he will... if
> you let us go now. Untie us...
> do it — before she comes out!

> STEWART
> (hesitates, then)
> We'll wait for Verna...

109   INT. EXAMINING ROOM   109

Verna is quite calm as she sits looking fondly at her
dead son.

> VERNA
> Just like your father... always
> getting into trouble wanting to
> do things on your own... I told
> your father, 'Billy,' I said,
> 'you're not man enough to drive
> a truck; you should be in business;
> putting your money in a health
> club with me to run it.' So
> what did he do? — Got behind
> the wheel of that smelly thing
> and ran that rig right off a
> cliff one rainy night. You're
> the same way, headstrong,
> always fighting me, wanting to
> do things your way. Till things
> go wrong, that is. Then it's
> always: 'Mom, help me...'
> (moves to him)
> All right, darling boy. You just
> rest yourself awhile. And don't
> worry, mother'll take care of
> everything. Just like she always
> has.

Then, after bending to kiss his forehead, Verna looks
up, her thoughts turning to revenge...

110   INT. WAITING ROOM - DAY   110

As Verna enters, staring grimly at Oxford.

(CONTINUED)

                         VERNA
              Stewart... I want you to point
              the gun at that man and shoot
              him.

The air is suddenly charged.

                         OXFORD
              Hey, now... Hold on...

                         BETTY
              No! Don't listen to her...

Stewart looks at Verna, bewildered.

                         VERNA
              You heard me swear it...
                    (to Oxford)
              ... If you let him die... you
              die.
                    (to Stewart)
              Do it!

                         BETTY
              Stewart, listen to me. Aren't
              you in enough trouble without
              adding murder to it?!

He hesitates. Verna regards him with contempt:

                         VERNA
              Stewart... aren't you ever going
              to be a man? — Just once?

Betty, working to free her hands, tries desperately to
stall him:

                         BETTY
              That's right, Stewart, be a man
              for once. Don't let her throw
              away your life the way she threw
              away her son's...

                         VERNA
                    (as if stabbed)
              After him... her! Shoot them
              both — !
                    (beat)
              Stewart — !

Stewart again hesitates.

111 INSERT - BETTY'S WRISTS   111

need only another tug or two to break free.

112 RESUME SCENE   112

as an enraged Verna moves to take the gun from Stewart:

                              VERNA
                    Me! It's always left for me to
                    get things done — !

113 INSERT - BETTY'S WRISTS   113

breaking free of the tape.

114 RESUME SCENE   114

Verna is yanking the gun out of Stewart's hand as Betty,
lightning fast, takes hold of a small wooden magazine
rack, and flings it at —

115 VERNA   115

who instinctively throws her hands up to ward off the
rack, and in so doing loses hold of the gun. As it
goes skittering on the floor —

116 BETTY   116

rushes to the gun and picks it up.

117 RESUME SCENE   117

As Betty turns, leveling the gun at them.

                              BETTY
                    All right... Let's all be nice
                    and calm... Stewart... untie the
                    doctor... When he does, Doc,
                    call the police...

When Stewart makes a move to comply, Verna takes hold
of his arm, restraining him:

                              VERNA
                    She's not going to use that gun.
                    Take it away from her.

                                              (CONTINUED)

                              BETTY
                           (tensing)
                 Don't try it, Stewart.   Untie him!

Stewart is frozen, caught between two imperatives.

                              VERNA
                           (at Betty)
                 That's the kind of man I always
                 wind up with; jelly for spines
                 and brains to match...

She is drawing out of her dress pocket the long surgical scissors she used earlier... and takes a menacing
step towards Betty...

118   ANOTHER ANGLE   118

     Betty's hand begins to tremble and she has to steady
     the gun with both of her hands.

                              BETTY
                 Stay back, Verna...

She retreats a step as Verna moves slowly toward her.

                              BETTY
                           (continuing)
                 Please, Verna... don't make me
                 shoot you...

119   INTERCUT STEWART AND OXFORD   119

     frozen, wide-eyed.

                              VERNA
                 You're like him... weak. You
                 don't have it in you to pull
                 that trigger.

                              BETTY
                 Yes, I do... I will...

And even as she says it, she is torn by doubt as to
whether or not she can. Meanwhile, Verna looms
closer.

                              OXFORD
                 Do it, lady!

                                                    (CONTINUED)

179

                              STEWART
                    Verna — !

                              OXFORD
                    If she gets that gun away from
                    you, she'll kill us both. Shoot
                    her — !!

120   EXT. DOCTOR'S BUNGALOW - DAY   120

           The car brakes to a stop. Barnaby and J.R. get out,
           start for the front door.

121   RESUME IN THE WAITING ROOM   121

           Betty takes a final step, her back now to the wall.

                              BETTY
                    Please... don't make me...

122   VERNA   122

           raises the scissors, readies for the final lunge...

123   ON BETTY   123

           FOCUSING ON the gun in her trembling hand. Then ADJUST
           FOCUS TO Betty. The pain of having to shoot or not
           shoot without another moment to spare narrows her eyes
           into excruciating slits.

124   EXT. FRONT DOOR - DAY   124

           As Barnaby and J.R. reach the threshold, and J.R.
           tries the door and finds it locked, they hear:

                              BETTY (O.S.)
                    Verna... No!

           At this, J.R. steps back, then rams his body against
           the door —

125   INT. WAITING ROOM   125

           As the door bursts open, Barnaby rushes past J.R. to-
           wards Verna. She turns on him, raising the scissors
           to strike. Barnaby takes hold of her wrist and re-
           lieves her of the weapon.

is in shock, still holding the gun up with both hands,
still pointing it at where Verna stood before Barnaby's
intercession. She shakes uncontrollably as J.R. moves
in.

> J.R.
> Betty... It's all over...

He says quietly as he gently takes the gun from her.

127   WIDER ANGLE   127

Verna sinks into a chair. Stewart sits by her, takes
her hand comfortingly. She pulls it free. Glares at
him. J.R. is crossing to untie Oxford, passing Barnaby,
who moves over to Betty.

> JONES
> You all right?

She nods, manages a smile, then buries herself in his
arms...

> CUT TO:

128   EXT. BARNABY'S OFFICES - NIGHT (STOCK)   128

129   INT. BARNABY'S OFFICE - NIGHT   129

Betty is seated, still unnerved by the day's events.
Barnaby fishes a bottle out of a cabinet, wipes off
the dust.

> JONES
> Remember the last time I gave you
> some of this old brandy?

> BETTY
> When I was hurting so badly from
> that toothache...?

> JONES
> (nodding)
> Want to see if it works again?

> (CONTINUED)

                         BETTY
          No, thanks, Barnaby. It's a
          different kind of hurt this time...
          That woman... If you and J.R.
          hadn't shown up when you did, I...

                         JONES
          It's something you better come
          to terms with right now, and
          not let it haunt you. Would
          you have been able to pull that
          trigger?

                         BETTY
          No! I couldn't...
                    (reconsiders)
          ... I guess that's what I'd like
          to think. But, yes... I guess I
          would have shot her. And that's
          why I'm hurting. Because the
          Vernas of this world make you
          realize that — given the
          circumstances...

Shrugs sadly.

130   ANOTHER ANGLE   130

J.R. comes breezing in; gestures at bottle:

                         J.R.
          Hey, hey, hey — don't leave it
          in the locker room, Betty. It's
          champagne tonight.
                    (to Barnaby)
          I made reservations at the Lucky
          Rooster for eight-thirty. We can
          just make it.

                         JONES
                    (impressed)
          The Lucky Rooster, huh? —

                         BETTY
          Pretty fancy.

                         JONES
          Sure you can afford a high class
          place like that, J.R.?

                                        (CONTINUED)

                         J.R.
               Me? Every time we all go out
               together, I pick up the tab
               one time, you pick it up the
               next. Isn't that the deal we
               made?

                         JONES
               Uh-huh. That's the deal.

                         J.R.
                    (recalls)
               That's right... You paid the check
               last Tuesday, didn't you?

They stir to go.

                         BETTY
                    (smiles)
               Still want to take us to the
               Lucky Rooster?

                         J.R.
                    (the sport)
               Sure, why not...? Who says I
               have to have breakfasts,
               lunches or dinners for the rest
               of the week anyway...?

Laughing as they exit, and we...

                                        FADE OUT.

                         THE END

8

Resolution

The final essential ingredient in writing your script is the effective resolution. The resolution should be logical and natural so the viewer does not ask, Now where did that come from? The resolution should fit, but it should not be telegraphed. Viewers should not be able to guess by what means the resolution will be brought about. Of course, in a detective show, audiences will expect the detective or police lieutenant to solve the case, but the means—the twists and turns—will be the surprises, but logical ones. The clues and hints that are sprinkled throughout a script or that appear only one time, depending on the type of story, are utilized in every category of writing.

CREATING CREDIBILITY

In an episode titled "Roper's Niece" in the television show "Three's Company" (written by George Burditt and Paul Wayne before the Ropers spun off into a separate short-lived series), a chain that Janet wears tangles with Jack's shirt. While Jack tries to work it loose, Janet tells him of the beautiful cameo that had been suspended from it. The cameo is now in a hockshop, she explains. She had hocked it to pay the rent. As part of the eventual happy solution, Jack presents Janet with her cameo. He had bought it back from the pawnshop with the fifty dollars Roper had given him to take his visiting niece out that night. But Jack had not spent the money on entertainment. His car was stalled on the freeway; he and the niece hadn't gone anywhere.

If no mention of the cameo had been made earlier in the episode, the cameo would have been too much of a surprise to the viewer. Where did the cameo come from? To the viewer it would have come out of left field. Its sudden introduction at the end of the script would have looked contrived. However, the introduction of the cameo earlier through mention of it gives credibility to its actual appearance in the resolution.

The Plant

The introduction of the cameo earlier in the script so that it does not come in later as a strange object of total surprise to the viewer is known as *planting*. The catching of the chain on Jack's shirt is skillful planting of the piece of jewelry, at least through mention of it. Remember: The sudden appearance of something that has a key place in the resolution of the script is contrived unless an earlier reference is made to fit. A plant can be an object (like the cameo), a character trait, or a part of the environment—whatever is needed in the resolution of your teleplay or screenplay in a natural way if it is to be a logical, credible part of your resolution.

In a "Columbo" television episode concerning the death in a car explosion of a news reporter, Columbo, investigating the case, questions a movie actress (played by Anne Baxter) in the living room of her apartment, which is located on a movie lot. The location had once been a movie set. During the interrogation the sharp-eyed Columbo notices that the fountain on the grounds outside the glass doors of the living room is dry. To his question as to why there is no water in the fountain, the actress answers with a casual shrug that the fountain fits the make-believe world of the movies and movie set in which she lives.

The viewer accepts this explanation easily. It is fitted into the script in a natural, logical way. As well as the home viewer accepting the credible explanation for the dry fountain, Columbo lets the subject go without another question. The viewer, accepting the logical explanation, is satisfied that Columbo appears to accept it, too.

But this is Columbo—relentless in his pursuit of the truth. His turning up a succession of clues illuminates the truth, and so solves the case. Eighteen years before, the fictitious movie star in the "Columbo" episode murdered her husband. The body is buried under the fountain. To set the water to play in the fountain, workmen would have had to dig under it and would have discovered the corpse. Thus, the fountain—its lack of water—proves to be an essential ingredient in the solution of a murder. The fountain is a plant. The scriptwriter skillfully gave Columbo a plausible opportunity to call attention to it so that when Columbo solves the murder, the digging up of the body buried under the fountain is acceptable to the viewer. The explanation of why it had not been found before left no gnawing doubt. Columbo could then go ahead and solve the crime.

In *One Flew Over the Cuckoo's Nest* another fountain plays a vital part in the resolution. The Indian inmate of large frame and strong body bursts out of the shackles of his mind, rips the water fountain off the floor of the mental institution, crashes it through a window, and follows it in his own leap outside. His running—with the camera following him in long shot until he disappears over the horizon—is a joyous, thrilling event on screen, both for the big Indian and for the audience.

Now, a water fountain is a natural part of a building frequented by or lived in by many people. Its presence in a mental institution is not odd. People drink water from a fountain. That is natural. But because it is a particularly big, heavy fountain and plays such a dynamic, vital role—the object used as the means for one to flee the mental institution (*One Flew Over the Cuckoo's Nest* is a superb title)—a sudden appearance of that fountain for the final scene would cause an audience to wonder where it came from.

In that case its sudden introduction would have looked contrived and so spoiled that wonderful ending. The heavy weight of the fountain needed to be planted, too, to make the ripping of it off its foundation by the strong and liberated Indian all the more the enthralling moment it proves to be.

This is taken care of early in the script. McMurphy (Jack Nicholson) makes a bet with his fellow inmates that he can lift the fountain. The bet is the indomitable McMurphy's answer to their challenge. But for all his strong determination and muscular straining, he cannot budge the fountain. The facts of its existence, weight, and immobility are planted early in the script in a natural way. The scene with the challenge of the fountain fits McMurphy's cockiness well, too, with just enough humor to enhance the naturalness.

You can see that a sudden introduction of the fountain and the heaviness that shows its immobility would make the Indian inmate's wrenching it off the floor and heaving it through the window less effective.

All the greater is the triumph of his liberation when he lifts the fountain and crashes it out the window. The choice of the fountain as his means of escape is marvelously dramatic, especially in a visual sense. Since this is a visual medium, it is the *sight* of the object or whatever else is the plant, that should be the most effective. The viewer can miss a line of dialogue, but he will remember the sight of something when it emerges as a key to the resolution.

A word of caution: Fit in whatever you need as the plant naturally, and do not overemphasize through repetition, or it can serve to telegraph its later application. You don't want the viewer to think, I know that fountain (or whatever else) is going to be part of the solution because the writer keeps reminding me to keep it in mind. The viewer would then be pre-guessing you, and that is fatal to the success of the script, teleplay, or motion picture. Remember: If the plant is obtrusive, the audience is likely to think that it will figure in the resolution. Do not telegraph your ending through overlabeling the specific ingredients you will need. However, at the other extreme, omission of the ingredients will give your resolution a contrived look, causing the viewer to ask that equally fatal question, Where did that come from?

In Henrik Ibsen's great play *Hedda Gabler* (filmed many times, with the latest version starring Glenda Jackson), the fireplace is an important element of the tragedy. At the peak of crisis, Hedda burns an important manuscript on the hearth. This action is vital to the drama in its powerful solution. It molds the character of Hedda and her destructive nature. She needs to destroy that manuscript. The most effective and visual way is to burn it. To effect this, Ibsen has left nothing to chance or an out-of-left-field introduction; no one asks, Where did that come from? This great and impeccable dramatist not only placed a fireplace in the living room (indeed, a natural part of a Scandinavian house because of the cold winters indigenous to that climate), but he made certain that audiences would know that the hearth was lit.

Early morning of the final and crucial day, Hedda tells the maid who is serving her breakfast to light a fire in the hearth. Ibsen left nothing to chance. Like the fire, the pistol that Hedda uses for her suicide does not just suddenly appear. An earlier reference is made to it as one of a set of pistols in the house.

Two plants are deftly laced into an excellent television feature film (movie of the week), *You'll Never See Me Again,* teleplay adaptation by William Wood and Gerald DiPego, adapted from a story by the late Cornell Woolrich, who was noted for his mystery-suspense novels and short stories. The plants are vital to the resolution involving a husband's desperate attempt to find his wife, who has suddenly disappeared. In trying to pick up her trail, he goes to the home of his wife's mother and her husband (the wife's stepfather) and questions them on when they last saw their missing daughter. The husband (protagonist) is meeting the mother and stepfather for the first time. It is at this time that he learns—and the audience learns, too—that the stepfather, a strapping man, built the house. This is his work and plant 1 of the film. Plant 2 is the passing information, laced neatly into the script, that the husband is an architect. Let's see how these two plants mesh into the script and carry the telefilm into high suspense resolution.

Although the mother and stepfather claim that they have not seen or heard from the daughter and have no information about where she could be, the missing woman's husband picks up a trail that leads him right back to that house on a second visit. At the time the husband picks up the new and significant information, the script has built to the point of no return for him—the strongest crisis where all seems lost: The search for his wife has dead-ended. Now hope subsides again. The couple still deny having seen her. It is at this point that the two plants, fitted naturally and unobtrusively into the script, serve good purpose.

Just as the husband is turning away in disappointment, he notices the wall paneling is uneven. Now, it is planted in the script that he is an architect: He has an eye trained to detect asymmetrical details in construction. That there can be such an error in construction is also logical. The audience recalls (plant 1) that the construction of the house was not a professional job. Therefore, the audience can accept the asymmetry of the panel as a natural human error. The combination of the use of both plants spurs the husband, knowing that something is wrong with the wall, to rip out the paneling. The result is intensely dramatic—a shocker. The body of a woman is discovered in the wall.

The viewer's first reaction is that this is the corpse of the missing wife. But here the script takes a new twist that plunges it into new suspense and builds into the final thrilling moments.

The body in the wall is that of the real mother. She had died, and the stepfather married the woman who is now posing as the mother of the missing young woman. The misuse of the identity enables the couple to come into a substantial amount of money that otherwise would be the property of the dead woman. Having stopped by to visit her mother, the daughter discovered the impersonation and was taken prisoner. The completion of the resolution is her husband's rescue of her. The film is an absorbing one, suspenseful with that body-in-the-wall twist that exposes the antagonist scheme. That exposé was highly visual, dramatic, and natural. But without the plants the asymmetrical construction of the wall and the husband's ability to recognize that error in building would not have been credible. The viewer would not accept that this could happen. It took the two plants to make the discovery of the corpse in the wall a natural one.

Characterization

Character traits can also play an important part in bringing about a resolution. *The Caine Mutiny* (screenplay adapted from the novel by Herman Wouk) is climaxed by the trial of Captain Queeg, who has a nervous habit of rolling little metal balls in his fingers. As the trial progresses, he becomes increasingly nervous. He rolls the little metal balls faster. The sound becomes conspicuous. All other sounds in the courtroom stop. The sound of the metal balls gets to Queeg. It points out that the nervousness is of a highly neurotic degree. Queeg breaks down. The nervous habit has triggered the resolution. But it must be pointed out that this, as in all use of plants, is an adjunct to the characterization.

Endowing the character with a special trait can give that trait usefulness in driving the story forward to the resolution. Queeg's habit is visible *but* not conspicuous and is accepted as a natural part of his characterization. Because it is so well woven into the characterization, it does not do what otherwise could be fatal to a story—telegraph the ending.

Plant what you need for the ending, but do not put a sign on it. If a plant is overemphasized, the viewer will likely guess the ending. Do not telegraph. No audience wants to be a step ahead of the writer of the script.

Do not telegraph, but on the other hand do not omit what you need to bring about the effective resolution, or you will have brought about a contrived and unsatisfying ending. An audience should not have to ask, Where did that come from? However, in the case of a character trait such as Queeg's, it blends in as part of the characterization and so does not become conspicuous.

Heaven Can Wait (screenplay by Warren Beatty and Elaine May, from *Here Comes Mr. Jordan*) introduces the protagonist (Warren Beatty) as a football player. Football is an important part of his life. But shortly after leaving the football field, where the audiences first meet him, he is killed in an accident. However, Mr. Jordan, the heavenly being (played by James Mason) who meets him at the pearly gates, tells him that he was not supposed to have died yet, although his body has already been cremated, and that he can be alive again if a living body is found for him. He is permitted to return to Earth to find that living person whose time is almost up.

A nearly dead man is a hapless husband whose wife and her lover think they have murdered him. However, he is not quite dead, and his body is taken over as the new body of the protagonist. Although he is recognized and accepted by the wife and her lover as the husband, to the audience he is the football player, enacted by Warren Beatty. Now, how can this protagonist look like one person, the football player, and yet be recognized as another, completely different, individual? Making the dual role plausible in this delightful comedy-fantasy is accomplished with a line of dialogue. Mr. Jordan tells the reincarnated football player that his appearance is unchanged except to those people who know him as the other identity. You can see what a well-placed line can do to make a screenplay work.

It also conveys to the audience the important fact that the mind and way of life of the football player remain the same. At heart, he is still the football player he was at the start. This fact is important to the resolution. The wife and her lover decide to try again to murder the man who to them is the husband. The wife's lover shoots him dead. Again to stay alive, he needs a body. Here is where the characterization of him as a football player serves its story line purpose by providing the resolution.

In the midst of the big game, the star player collapses. Mr. Jordan seizes the opportunity to have the hero step into the body of this football player before he dies. In his new identity on the football field, the hero wins the game for his team, and thus the motion picture also winds up with a happy ending.

The story fits together nicely. But think of the vital ingredients that had to be injected into the script to make it work—and it does work with a logic most acceptable to the comedy-fantasy.

Quite often, too—depending upon the material—the resolution evolves out of the actions of the characters without the need to employ some specific device. Neil Simon's *The Goodbye Girl* takes its characters through the paces of conflict, romance emerging from the conflict, and the breakup in which the Goodbye Girl again loses a man. But unlike his predecessors, this man promises that he will be back—and the audience and Pamela, the Goodbye Girl, are convinced that he means it. It is evident that he is sincerely in love with her and that she wants him. The emotional behavior of the characters, driving the script forward, determines the resolution.

In the Oscar-winning screenplay *Midnight Express,* Billy, the American jailed in Turkey on a drug-smuggling charge, is pushed to a breaking point where, in solitary confinement, he has lost all hope. Finally, while he is brutally beaten by a prison guard, he turns furiously on him, knocks him out, puts on his uniform, and escapes from prison. Because he is so low in spirits and so powerless to help himself, his sudden turnabout would appear implausible if it were not for a key scene that builds into acceptance of the challenge to save himself.

He has a visitor from home, and she tells him that if he doesn't do something to get out of the prison, he will die. When Billy turns on the guard, this is the spur by which he comes alive. It is believable that even in his most desperate state, the challenge would have impressed itself on him. But without the challenge, his sudden show of strength and the will to survive would not have been credible.

Bohannan, the protagonist of the teleplay "Bohannan" on "Gunsmoke" (which, lasting seventeen years, was the longest-running Western series on television), is a faith healer who sincerely believes he is helping people and is not practicing quackery. But the antagonist, a medical doctor in Dodge City (the locale of the show) who is treating the boy, Heck, for what he diagnoses as a fatal muscular disease, considers Bohannan a charlatan who must be stopped. However, Heck's mother desperately turns to Bohannan for help.

Bohannan is honest enough to believe that he does not have the power within himself to heal the boy. The boy will not live more than a year; yet the resolution is a satisfying one for Bohannan, Heck, and his mother, too.

What makes the resolution possible is the development in the script of the friendship between Bohannan and the boy. As the boy gets to know Bohannan, he listens, enthralled, to Bohannan's stories of the wonderful places he has visited in his travels. Heck wants to travel with Bohannan, visiting all those fascinating places. Heck's mother consents, and, of course, Bohannan is happy to take the lad along with him. It is not necessary for Heck to know that this is the last year of his life. All he knows is that this will be a joyous year for him. Indeed, this is a satisfying resolution and a credible one, with the plant for it the scene in which Bohannan enthralls Heck with the stories of his travels. That scene, too, is a natural one. The little boy wants to hear about those places that to him have a faraway enchantment.

A NATURAL BLENDING

The resolution in *The Sting,* David Ward's original screenplay, is one of stunning surprise. The shock value of the ending of this Oscar-winning motion picture is what appears to be the fatal shooting of the protagonist antihero (played by Paul Newman) by a syndicate man in a game of sting over sting. Here is the antihero protagonist falling dead, his blood and his life oozing out of him. But after the antagonist and his associates leave the scene, satisfied that he is dead, he leaps to his feet whole and alive. Audiences are startled and delighted. This is a marvelous joke. The joke is thoroughly believable, too. But here, contrary to planting the possibility of a joke, nothing in the script gives any indication that such a plan is being set. You may ask, then, how this joke could come off with such believability.

Although there is no audience preparation for the joke, the screenplay contains no false note. Throughout the film, the audience knows what is happening only when it happens. If each move designed to play against the opposition were explained before being put into operation, the divulging of the shooting plan would have been obligatory, too. Otherwise, the screenplay would look out of joint. If the audience were let in on all the other moves before they were put into effect, this last one with the surprise twist would have had to be explained, too, to fit the

entire pattern of the writing. Of course, such advance preparation would have canceled out the marvelous joke. But the
economy of the writing that divulged nothing of any plan until it
was put into effect gave the holding back on the truth of the
shooting its believability—and its surprise.

This type of technique was also employed in the segments of
the television series "Mission Impossible" as part of the format
of the show. To accomplish the assigned mission, instructions
were given to each principal on the role each was to play. But
nothing that each would do in carrying out the mission to a
successful conclusion was divulged ahead of time. The viewer
saw each principal in action, and that was self-explanatory.

Remember, then: Whatever resolution you want for your
teleplay or screenplay, make certain it blends into your work as
a natural part of it. The resolution should not alter the pace or
pattern of the writing or inject a sour note. In the suspense-
thriller or murder-mystery, if that should be your inclination,
avoid the red herring, or false clue that is a false lead having
nothing to do with the rest of the story and that is not again
even referred to. The red herring should be avoided in any other
type of writing, too, whether comedy or drama. An emphasis on
one person, place, or thing that has no real connection with the
story is another type of false lead. The story gives expectations
of something emerging from that emphasis but, instead, drops
the subject.

On the other hand, writing that overemphasizes and so
telegraphs the resolution is not good form either. If something is
stressed repeatedly in the script, making an audience certain that
it must be vital in the resolution, then when it does prove to be
the specific factor in the solution the ending can be so unsatisfying that it gives the audience a feeling of having been cheated
for having been able to guess the ending.

In a segment of the television series "Kaz," the attorney
protagonist (star of the series) tries desperately to have a
psychiatric report concerning a client admitted into evidence.
This report is vital to the attorney's defense of his client. His
attempts are futile. Not only does the judge refuse to admit the
report into evidence, but every time the word *psychiatric* is

mentioned, the judge becomes furious. So overwrought is the judge that he even orders the attorney jailed for contempt of court for his insistence over the psychiatric report. The judge's overreaction to any suggestion of psychiatry is a telegraphing of the resolution.

Investigation by the attorney leads to the information that the judge had been a patient in a sanitarium. The judge breaks down when the attorney confronts him with his past confinement. The attorney wins his case, while the judge is a surefire candidate for another stay in the sanitarium. Here is a telegraphed resolution. It could have been printed on the screen: It became extremely obvious that the judge's burst of fury at any mention of psychiatry indicated that it touched him personally. The overwrought condition he displayed pointed up a deep-seated psychosis in him.

To compound the teleplay's weakness, midway through it a young woman investigator for the attorney tells him that she has found out something. He had sent her to check on the judge's background. However, the attorney is too busy at that moment to hear her out; she will have to tell him later what she learned. Leaving information dangling is another form of red herring, a kind of bait that does nothing but try a viewer's patience over having to wait to find out something. The pertinent information that the attorney postpones hearing is that the judge had been in a sanitarium. Of course, if the lawyer had allowed the investigator to tell him earlier in the script—at the time she wanted to tell him—it would have been obligatory for him to confront the judge at this early point in time. That confrontation would have brought the script to its conclusion before the hour was up. It is delayed, while the Johnny-one-note of psychiatry is being featured and so telegraphing the obvious resolution. There is no variation on the reference to psychiatry and the judge's anger over it. It has too obvious a place in the script.

Repetition does not always mean telegraphing of the resolution. As described earlier, the nervous finger play of Captain Queeg in *The Caine Mutiny* causes his breakdown at the trial. But the little nervous finger play of the captain does not telegraph the resolution. There are other pressing factors in the trial interrogation that are pushing him into the breakdown. The accelerated roll of the metal balls accentuates that he is on the verge of collapse, but it is not a Johnny-one-note. When one element in a script is emphasized repeatedly and that element turns out to be the single factor resolving the story, then and only then has it been telegraphed.

Kramer vs. Kramer, the Oscar-winning motion picture, reaches its resolution through the character of the wife, who sues Kramer for custody of her little boy. She wins the custody suit, but she does give up the little boy to his father because she knows that she cannot handle the responsibility. Her characterization shows a lack of stability, and this is borne out in her interrogation by Kramer's attorney in the custody trial. Asking her about the endurance of her relationships with men, he draws out from her that she has not sustained any. It is natural for her to realize, when faced with the sole custody of her little son, that she cannot handle such responsibility. This is a satisfying ending, because what started out as strong hostility of the boy toward his father has developed into love for him. In turn, Kramer has a deep love for his son.

Note that although the wife does not play a strong role after she walks out on Kramer, she is the antagonist who strikes at the same time that Kramer and his boy are relating with tremendous love. Additionally, note that it is the conflict of the boy and Kramer (brought about by the boy's resentment of his father) that builds the story line to the heightened drama of the custody suit. However, up to that point the wife is shown at intervals in a store across the street, watching the little boy through the window. The camera picks her up; the audience is never allowed to forget her. This fine screenplay also earned the screenwriter, Robert Benton, an Oscar.

In the mystery-detective genre, clues are important in effecting the resolution and solving a case. A teleplay or screenplay detective who picks up an important clue and fails to divulge its contents until sometime later, perhaps at the denouement—the final outcome—is likely to exasperate a viewer (if the show even reaches the screen). Viewers must not be cheated. Although the audience should not keep pace with the deductions the clever detective makes as the clues pile up, information should not be withheld or given the red herring treatment. The detective must always be one jump ahead of the viewer, or he cannot live up to the reputation he should have to stay alive on the screen as a brilliant solver of crimes. The detective will put it all together.

In *Murder on the Orient Express,* the audience is presented with clues and motivations of suspects for committing the crime. The brilliant Belgian provides the superb murder solution. Poirot and his extraordinary little gray cells deliver the superb murder solution—a spectacular surprise, though a credible one, because pieces of the puzzle are shown to the audience as the great detective uncovers them. But, certainly, it is Poirot who fits them together.

In the early stages of a murder investigation in a "Columbo" segment, Columbo notices broken glass on the floor near the corpse. When nailing down the murderer, he names the murder weapon as a microscope with which the murderer struck his victim a lethal blow on the head. The heavy blow shattered the glass and thus accounts for the splintered glass Columbo observes. This observation provides an essential plant for solving the crime, just as the fountain that plays no water is a pertinent plant for the episode described earlier.

In pure character drama and comedy, the resolution may be worked out entirely through characterization and conflicts of the story line. In the motion picture *Love and Pain and the Whole Damn Thing,* the protagonist (played by Maggie Smith) at intervals stumbles or even falls. It is usually a light fall that seems to imply that she has tripped. Later, however, serving as an important part in the resolution, is the revelation that she is suffering from a fatal illness. Her romantic involvement with a young man years her junior creates the conflict of the drama; their quarrels climax with their breaking up their relationship. Their subsequent reunion and decision to live together for the rest of her days is impelled by her fatal illness.

The earlier spills she takes do not telegraph that she is terminally ill—a condition that at the time she is not aware of any more than is the audience. But when her fatal illness becomes known, it is natural and logical because of her earlier moments of physical unsteadiness. Now, this is not a plant. It is not one item set into the film to be remembered at the resolution. The little spills she takes are more of a foreshadowing of things to come.

Whatever the plant or foreshadowing you find you need for the resolution, make certain that the resolution is natural, logical, and yet not telegraphed. Remember, too, that whatever you place into the script—deftly woven into it—must be there for a purpose. Anton Chekhov made the observation that the writer who sets a loaded gun on stage at the beginning of the play must make certain that it is fired before the play ends.

Ibsen did not set the pistol in Hedda Gabler's living room for wall decoration, or a fire in the hearth because it looks pretty.

9

The Page Form—Camera Shots

Now that you have studied the component parts of an effective script, we continue with the page form in terms of the writer's role in applying camera terms to the script. It is the director who determines every setup and numbers every one of them on the shooting script. (In camera terms, each such shot is a new setup.) Your job is to write and not be encumbered by a multiplicity of camera shots likely to be changed by the director. Use master shots.

MASTER SHOTS

What are master shots? They are the basic ones, mainly the placing of the characters in the scenes they play. For example, when your scene opens on the Dallings in the kitchen (see Chapter 2), you have placed them in a master shot. During their exchange of dialogue, you would be encumbering your script if you tried to call the camera shots on each of the Dallings.

For example, you may visualize a close shot on Joe Dalling in a heated moment of conflict between him and his wife. But the director may want the close shot on Mrs. Dalling, or he may decide that a close shot is unnecessary for either of them. If you wish, during a stretch of dialogue you may write the word INTERCUT on the left side of the page. This and all other directions involving camera work are typed in capital letters. However, if a camera shot is vital to your script—if its emphasis is of genuine importance to the story you are telling—include the camera shot. For example, a strange and sinister face peers through the window. It is vital to your script that the viewer see this face before a murder is committed. You need a CLOSE-SHOT of the face. By all means, specify. To illustrate:

```
CLOSESHOT:  A face, peering through the window—a man's face of
any year and any place.  The face is hard to decipher because of
the strange and satanic look that stamps him as indeterminate in
years and not belonging to Earth.
```

The description can be bone thin or more embellished, but not beyond what you mean to convey.

Other camera shots may also be necessary to clarify the position of your characters. Let us select another argumentative couple: Harold and Julie. But they are not alone. As they are engaged in a heated argument in the garden outside their home, Tom approaches, saying, "Why don't you two put on the gloves?" How do you handle Tom's entrance in the scene? A simple camera direction that neatly handles Tom's arrival is:

```
ANGLE ON:  To include Tom as he enters the garden and joins
Harold and Julie.
```

Used judiciously, ANGLE ON is a handy camera term that does not clutter the page with intricacies that could annoy the director, should the script get past the purchase stage and into production. Also, a busy story editor (and aren't they all?) might become impatient enough with pages overburdened with camera shots to abandon further reading of the script.

Again, we emphasize that the writer's use of camera shots is confined chiefly to master shots, with the sole exception of those essential to the script—those that for the sake of story must be written into the screenplay or teleplay.

TECHNICAL CAMERA TERMS

The following camera terms may be so essential to the telling of your story that you must include them.

A PAN (panoramic) SHOT is camera work that traverses an area, moving across it. The PAN may be used as an establishing shot, to set the type of area, but always be sure that it is an essential PAN for the telling of your story. If you feel such a panoramic shot is important in that respect, include it. A director can always cut it out.

An example is the PAN SHOT early in the feature film *Brian's Song*. The camera pans the football field to show the players in football practice. Then Gale Sayers, a major character in the film, arrives in a taxi. The PAN SHOT not only has established the football motif so vital to the story, but it tells the audience immediately that Sayers is showing up late, after the practice has begun.

POV in camera terms stands for *point of view*. For example, if your character Harold needs to catch the reaction of Julie over something he has said or done, you can designate as a camera shot:

POV—Harold to Julie.

And if Julie needs to catch Harold's reaction, the camera cue is:

REVERSE SHOT—Julie to Harold.

POV and REVERSE SHOT should be applied judiciously, again only when imperative for your story.

Under certain circumstances you will need to include directives to clarify your script. One is the use of the term O.S., meaning off scene. For example, if one of your characters speaks but is not yet on the scene, you will need to let the audience know from where the voice comes. Let's go back to Tom, who enters the garden and joins Harold and Julie. Suppose that before he enters the garden, he speaks the line, "Why don't you two put on the gloves?"

In your script the off-scene directive should be included beside the name of the character, in parentheses.

```
                  TOM (O.S.)
        Why don't you two put on the gloves?
```

However, if your script calls for an off-scene voice that functions to set the mood, the locale, or the theme, or to bridge transitions, the voice is serving as the *narrator*. In that case, you write in the narrator's voice as V.O. The V.O. is also in parentheses, placed beside the word NARRATOR, as in the following:

```
                NARRATOR (V.O.)
        This is a story of two young people
        who think that they are in love, but
        discover to their amazement—
```

```
                    or—
```

```
                NARRATOR (V.O.)
        At midnight in the little town of
        Elmira, the main street is dark and
        deserted.  The street lamps blinked
        off two hours ago—
```

A few teleplays and screenplays carry a narrator throughout who serves the dual purpose of bridging time and mood sequences and underscoring certain significant advances in the story. But the use of the narrator is infrequent and should be employed if the story can only be told in that manner. Otherwise, the interjection of a narrator can impede the flow of continuity.

CUES TO THE ACTOR

There are also directives that you may wish to write into your script to cue the actor. To illustrate, one of your characters pauses during his dialogue before he continues speaking. The pause is defined on the typewritten page as "beat." Beat should be in parentheses: (beat).

If emotions expressed by characters as they speak are pertinent and you want to be sure of their special emphasis, any description of these emotions should be set in parentheses:

```
                    JULIE
          (in a fury) You think I care if
          you walk out on me?  I'm jumping
          with joy!  Get out—and don't
          forget your toothbrush!

                    HAROLD
          (tenderly) I didn't mean it,
          darling.  I love you, and I'll
          prove it to you.  (beat)  I'm
          going to put the cap back on the
          toothpaste!
```

Note that Harold pauses (beat) before he delivers the line that he hopes will placate Julie.

As a general directive to you, keep actors' cues, like camera shots, at a minimum. Have faith in an actor's skill in interpreting the lines and in your well-written script conveying what you mean.

Remember: Don't try to do the director's job. Concentrate on your primary work—writing.

10

The Work Method

Structuring the script is the most difficult part of the writing. This is an opinion shared by both writers and story editors in the industry. The teleplay and screenplay are disciplined forms of writing. They require a blueprint that in its final stage becomes the treatment, or the scene-by-scene breakdown in narrative form, before you write the complete script. Once you have set the treatment and know how your story progresses scene by scene, your blueprint is ready to be transposed into the complete script—complete with the dialogue and action that is called for on each complete script page.

PREPARATION

Before you have written your treatment, you must have first worked out your story. Set down your story in narrative form, emphasizing your plot points and highlighting the story in consecutive action with the essential beginning, middle, and end.

The outline can be fuller, with more flesh than the bare bones of a synopsis. However, you should consult it only as the organization of the story you want to tell, and as a way of knowing that you have thought it out sufficiently to go on to the next stop— the treatment, or scene-by-scene blueprint of your script.

But where does your entire creative process begin? It starts with your basic idea, or plot capsule. You should be able to tell yourself what your idea is in three or four lines. The three or four lines—the plot capsule—must contain those basic elements that have been set forth in detail in previous chapters; namely, the protagonist with the objective that must be obtained, the antagonist setting the obstacles in the way of achieving that goal, the buildup to the most critical point for the protagonist (point of no return), and the resolution.

Shape the raw material of your idea with these basic elements. Be certain of the story you want to tell, and be sure that it contains these essential ingredients. Once you are certain you have the capsule of the story you want to tell, then you can work on outlining it and further blueprint your outline into treatment. At that point you are ready to write your full teleplay or screenplay. Working your idea in this step-by-step fashion can save you the mistake of starting to write from a springboard that lacks the essentials. Structuring is most important; it is the basis of your writing.

CHECKLIST FOR YOUR WRITING

When I first started teaching television and motion picture writing, I devised a checklist for students that they find very helpful in setting their plot capsule and from it building their outline, treatment, and—as the final step—writing the full script.

Check out whether you have these elements in your work. You will find it helpful to write down the answers to the basic questions in this checklist. If you find that you have difficulty in answering some of the questions in clear-cut terms, then consider that you may have unclear elements in your story structuring. It is best that you review your work and make sure that you can answer these questions. Write down the answers, because then you will know for certain that your script is structured effectively.

1. Who is your protagonist?
2. What does your protagonist want—with an urgency? What is the protagonist objective—something desperately wanted?
3. Who is your antagonist?
4. Why does your antagonist want to stop your protagonist?
5. Do you have good motivation for your protagonist objective, and is it in character with the protagonist?
6. Do you have the motivation for your antagonist? (Remember: Even in the psycho-antagonist type of script—quite overdone—something sets the psycho off out of his own twisted thinking.)
7. Have you introduced the problem of protagonist versus antagonist well up front in the script?
   a. Is the conflict—major problem—under way before the end of your first teleplay act in a show of one hour or longer? The equivalent in timing for the screenplay?
   b. In the half-hour show, is the major problem—conflict— set up and under way in the first few minutes of the first act, or first half of the show?
8. Do you have a provocative hook to open your script?
9. Does your script build and continue to build, sustaining the thrust and counterthrust pattern of conflict—into the highest peak of crisis and complication for the protagonist—at the point of no return?
10. Does every scene and every act of your script build toward it?
11. Is there any scene that does not pertain to the problem—the conflict—of your story line?
12. If a scene does wander or divert from the story line, what do you do about it? Since this is a question going beyond your own analysis of your work, here are answers:
    a. Delete the scene entirely. If it diverts your story line, you don't want it in.
    b. However, you may have a good character touch or dialogue that you feel is pertinent to your script, even though the entire scene is unnecessary and only stalls the

progress of your story. In that case, what you want to preserve, you may be able to combine with another scene or scenes.

13. Once your script builds its suspense and interest to that point, how is your script resolved?
   a. Have you reached that point where your next scenes will carry your protagonist over the hump of the worst phase of the problem into the resolution?
   b. Have you given your protagonist the most challenging complication of all—the worst complication in terms of the trouble he's in?

14. For the resolution, ask yourself:
   a. Is the resolution natural, credible? Do you have the plant(s) or foreshadowing you may need to help provide the resolution that is logical?
   b. Or, is your resolution telegraphed? Are you overemphasizing a plant or foreshadowing so that the audience is tipped off to the solution?

Since these are basic elements in the writing of your teleplay or screenplay, your answers to the questions can tell you whether you are working on a solid foundation. If you feel vague about any of the answers—for example, if you do not have a clear-cut answer concerning your protagonist objective or the antagonist counteraction—then it is likely that your script will lack the conflict that is so essential to build the suspense and interest. Review and rewrite whatever you feel shows some weakness in the script. Be entirely satisfied that your script is your very best effort before you submit it.

MARKETING YOUR TELEPLAY OR SCREENPLAY

How do you market your work? This is a question every new writer asks, and sometimes prematurely, before even starting to write the script. First, the new writer must have a script, or there is no basis for marketing any material.

The Agent

How do you go about offering your script to market? The best approach is through an agent to act for you. Studios make it a policy not to accept unsolicited material (that is, material submitted directly by a writer). But how do I find an agent? you ask. Who are the agents?

The agent you want to market your script is an agent on the list the Writers Guild of America West provides. These are guild signatory agents, i.e., agents who abide by guild regulations and are signatories to the guild agreement covering agents. You can obtain the list of these agents for one dollar (free of charge to members) by writing to Writers Guild of America West, 8955 Beverly Blvd., Los Angeles, CA 90048, or by phoning (213) 550-1000.

Because the guild puts out new lists of agents quite frequently—sometimes once a month—it does not give permission for the reprinting of any given list of agents in a publication. The reason, I am told, is that new agents enter the business, thus changing the list; mergers also are not infrequent, with sometimes some of the biggest agents in the business combining forces.

How do you select an agent? A guideline is the asterisk before the names of agents on the guild list who will consider material from new writers. But that can be flexible, too. Persevere, and make your contacts personally. Once you have completed your script, phone or write an agent, describing the type of material you are offering (screenplay, feature for television, or series script). If you are a local phone call away from the agent, phoning is the more satisfying way. Never submit your work without an initial contact. Then, you will know that you are submitting your script to an agent who already expects your material. Always have a brief cover letter with your submission, that mentions your phone conversation with the agent or the letter that opened the door to your sending the script.

If you have a published story or book, or a play that has been produced, it could serve you well to mention them. Your play does not have to be produced on Broadway or in any major production. Little theaters are doing fine work throughout the country. If you have had a little theater production for a play, do not fail to mention it, particularly if your play has been well received by reviewers. After all, if you had a Broadway run for your play, you probably would not have to knock on doors to make that first agent reading contact. If you are published (stories or a book), mention that. But it's your script that will see you through.

The guild also publishes a market list of television shows in its monthly newsletter, *POV* (Point of View), available free to members. A nonmember can buy a *POV* for two dollars. Each show listed specifies whether it is an open or closed one for writers. You will find that most of the shows are designated as open for submissions made through agents.

Hints to Help Yourself

As a cue for you in respect to new television shows, it is advisable not to write for any new series show unless it is establishing a success. Otherwise, even before you finish your script, the new show might be canceled. You are on safer ground writing your script for the established series show or the two-hour feature film, which offers more than one market for a specific submission. The major networks offer features made for television, and pay-TV will likely increase the demand for original features, as well as open the way for new series shows.

The guild also offers a registration service for writers' scripts at 310 N. San Vicente, Los Angeles, CA (corner of San Vicente and Beverly boulevards, third floor). Office hours are from 10:00 to 12:00 and 2:00 to 5:00. The telephone number is (213) 655-2095; the registration fee for nonmembers of the guild is ten dollars and for guild members, four dollars. If you mail your script, enclose one copy with your fee and send it to Writers Guild of America West at the WGA Beverly Boulevard address. Your receipt will be mailed back, along with your registration number. The registration is good for ten years and is renewable.

Keep up with the entertainment news, too. Your favorite newspaper will likely publish the new weekly show ratings in its television section. If you can obtain *The Hollywood Reporter* or *Daily Variety*—the industry trade papers—you will find that they regularly report the ratings.

For screenplays, the hits are determined by the box office receipts and lines forming to buy tickets. You will know soon enough which movies have rocketed to success and which did not get out of the basement. Study them just as you must study—watch and study—the television shows, especially shows for which you want to write.

Learn your craft. Be critical of yourself. If after you reread your script, you are not satisfied and see that some changes should be made, by all means make the revisions before sending your material out. You want to present your best effort.

Remember: Much of writing is rewriting. Know your craft and work at it. Once you make that first sale, I recommend you join the guild, which functions as your union in television, motion pictures, and radio. Member writers within the framework of the guild automatically receive the guild contracts and other benefits in the industry. The fee to join is five hundred dollars; the sale of your script will more than reimburse you.

The rewards for the writer of television and motion picture scripts make it all worthwhile. With the greatly expanding markets, it is predicted that writers in this field who prove their scriptwriting capabilities will have almost incalculable opportunities. It is estimated that under the profit-sharing terms of the new contracts, if at least 30 million homes are equipped with pay-TV within the next ten years, with pay-TV grossing $10 million, a writer can earn $150,000 on one script in addition to the basic minimum fee. At one time such payments for writers could be looked upon as the writer's pipe dream. They are no longer pipe dreams, but a golden promise based upon the tremendously expanding popularity of the new entertainment technologies among consumers.

Writer, today is yours! The future is yours! But to establish yourself in television and motion pictures—to sell that first script—you must work for it—at your typewriter.

Good luck!

Index